THE
CULM VALLEY
LIGHT RAILWAY

~

MICHAEL MESSENGER

TWELVEHEADS PRESS

1993

Few photographs capture the rural setting of the Culm Valley branch as well as this view of 1451 crossing the end of Culmstock Bridge, returning to Tiverton Junction with loaded milk tanks on the 2.45 p.m. from Hemyock. 8 August 1962.
M. J. FOX

TWELVEHEADS PRESS

First published 1993 by Twelveheads Press,
Chy Mengleth, Twelveheads, Truro,
Cornwall TR4 8SN.

ISBN 0 906294 29 0
British Library Cataloguing-in-Publication Data.
A catalogue record for this book is available from the British Library.

Printed by The Amadeus Press Ltd.,
Huddersfield, Yorks.

CONTENTS

*At Hemyock on 24 August
1951. The two milk tanks have
been free wheeled from the milk
factory into the yard and the
engine has now picked them up
to attach to the front of the
train.*
R. J. SELLICK COLLECTION,
NATIONAL RAILWAY MUSEUM

INTRODUCTION

Devon is an immensely attractive county and, rightly so, receives many visitors. Since Brunel brought the broad gauge railway to South Devon many parts of the county have been dependent on the tourist industry but there are a few places that have escaped the influx. No matter how crowded the beaches of the English Riviera or the Golden Coast, to use the coinage of two generations of marketing men, there is always a quiet corner of Devon to be enjoyed. Some corners have evaded even the most assiduous modern tourist guide and, whilst not actually 'off the map', might as well

be for many visitors.

Ironically, one such quiet corner is touched briefly by both the M5 motorway and the London to Penzance main railway line so most people entering Devon pass within a few miles. A prosperous and industrious valley, but secluded, with few major tourist attractions, it has only a long forgotten novel by R. D. Blackmore (of Lorna Doone fame) to give it literary immortality.

This is the valley of the River Culm. The river rises in the Blackdown Hills, towards the Somerset border on the east, and heads west-

Climbing into the Crossways cutting and just about to pass under the A38 (former turnpike) road. Above 1449 can be seen the track dropping into the plain of the river Culm, illustrating the sharp curves so typical of the line. The low retaining wall to the left may be a reminder of the early problems of the cutting. 23 July 1958.
R. C. RILEY

At Tiverton Junction on 23 July 1958, 1449 attaches milk tanks from Hemyock to the rear of the 12.30 p.m. Penzance to Kensington milk train. The ultimate destination in London could be, for example, Wood Lane, West Ealing, Mitre Bridge or Cricklewood.

R. C. RILEY

wards to join the Exe near Stoke Canon, north of Exeter. In the process it has carved out a valley, not over wide and flanked by relatively high ground on both sides, but fertile.

Through this valley, for nearly a century, ran the Culm Valley Light Railway. In the later years of its life, when your author came to know it as the Culm Valley branch of British Railways, it was one of the delightful rail byways of England. It was a marked contrast to the nearby main line where, on summer Saturdays, a stream of holiday specials headed by powerful gleaming steam giants thundered westwards to populate the beaches of Devon and Cornwall.

In the Culm Valley one of the smallest classes of steam locomotive took a single elderly coach and, usually, a string of milk tank wagons up and down the line in a most leisurely and unhurried way. Curves abounded and it was widely held that this was because the line had had to be built around the sides of the fields. Passengers were few and milk was clearly the lifeline of the branch.

In retrospect this was, with a little variation, the story of the branch throughout its life. Such an insignificant line might be thought not worthy of study or not to have a history worth exploring. This is not the case, however. The Culm Valley Light Railway, to give it its formal title, was a pioneering railway. It was one of the earliest light railways, although not quite as early as the directors believed. Whilst it had no great ambitions for itself, it carried a torch which its founders expected to set rural transport alight throughout the country. It did not do so, alas, but did give the benefit of rail transport to the Culm Valley and, thanks to the pioneering efforts of another group of local men, brought economic benefits to the valley that have survived the railway.

The branch line, built to meet a nineteenth century need, eventually and inevitably succumbed to the twentieth century and closed a few months before its centenary. In its own distinctive way it served the Culm Valley well and for this alone deserves recording.

CHAPTER ONE

INCEPTION

'Light cheap railways will confer a benefit wherever they are introduced'.
THE BISHOP OF EXETER, 1873.

In the mid-nineteenth century the Culm Valley was in much the same transport situation as it is today, albeit without the internal combustion engine. It was literally off the beaten tracks of road or rail. By the eighteenth century agriculture had become the predominant industry and the River Culm and its tributaries supported many corn mills. Other industries also made use of the water power, and serge and paper mills were established.

William White, in 1850, described Uffculme as 'a decayed market town in the picturesque valley of the small river Culm' with a nearly obsolete weekly fair or market. A carrier ran to Tiverton. Culmstock and Hemyock were described respectively as 'large' and 'considerable' villages. The former too had lost its weekly fair. Murray's *Handbook for Travellers in Devon and Cornwall* in 1859 summed up the district:

> The Black Down Hills . . . embosom some secluded valleys and crystal trout-streams, and are intersected by innumerable narrow lanes.

The Grand Western Canal, from Taunton to Tiverton, touched the valley but probably made little difference. The Bristol & Exeter Railway reached Exeter, on the broad gauge, from Taunton in 1844, after a year's temporary halt at Beam Bridge, south west of Wellington. It supplanted much of the traffic on the Exeter turnpike, opened in the mid-1770s. Both road and railway passed through Willand parish where they joined the lower section of the Culm Valley and followed the river to Exeter.

The opening of the railway, like the turnpike before it, had little effect on the small Culm Valley towns of Culmstock, Uffculme and Hemyock. Their inhabitants looked to the market towns of Taunton, Wellington, Honiton and Tiverton. All bar the last meant a climb over the Blackdowns and, whilst the turnpikes and town roads may have been metalled, the influence of John Macadam had certainly not reached the local lanes and roads. Few were metalled and most were as good as the underlying strata and geology permitted them to be.

The railways were the transport wonder of the age and by the 1850s most of the national network was laid down, connecting nearly all the major centres. Smaller towns, which perhaps had originally resisted the vulgar railways, saw clearly their advantages and sought to be connected to the system, if only by a branch line. Often this was too late, for transport habits and patterns had soon been laid down by the early routes, and it was already becoming clear that many places would not generate sufficient traffic to justify the expense of a railway. If the major railway companies thought a line could be remunerative then they either built it or sponsored it, in one way or another. If not they were content to do nothing; to leave the job to a local company to take the risk and to leave local people to raise the capital for what they foresaw to be a loss-making enterprise. It would be cynical to say that if local optimism built the line they could always buy it up cheaply when it became a financial failure, but it often happened.

Another school of thought was germinating, though; the embryo light railway movement that was to grow and be a prominent, if unfulfilled, part of railway politics for the next fifty years. There was an expanding belief that where the traffic did not support it there was no need for a fully equipped railway line. A railway built to a lesser standard and operated accordingly would suffice; a light railway. Parliament made its first steps with the Railway

Construction Facilities Act of 1864 that permitted, in certain circumstances, a railway to be built without the necessity for an expensive individual act of parliament. The Regulation of Railways Act 1868 went further and permitted light railways by just three of its clauses. By authority of the Act the Board of Trade was enabled to authorise the construction and working of a light railway, subject to such conditions as the Board might make. Whilst there was no attempt to legally define a light railway the imposition of limits on axle weights of vehicles to eight tons and speeds to a maximum of 25 m.p.h. did create a subtle definition.

One of the early proponents of light railways was an engineer named Arthur Cadlick Pain. Although he was born at Battersea, London, his family were of west country origin, having roots in the Bridgwater area. He was educated at Winchester and after an engineering pupillage under the County Surveyor for Devon he spent a year as an assistant to W. R. Galbraith and R. P. Brereton. The latter was formerly Brunel's Chief Assistant and, at the time Pain was with him, Chief Engineer to the Great Western Railway. From 1866 Pain practised on his own account as an engineer and worked overseas. By the early 1870s he was working back in Devon, on the Exeter Waterworks and in the Teign Valley. He was also to be engineer of the Westleigh Tramway, a three feet gauge line linking Burlescombe Station, on the Bristol & Exeter Railway main line north east of Tiverton Junction, with nearby stone quarries.*

In October 1871, when only 27 years of age, Pain approached Henry S. Ellis with a suggestion of a novel railway up the Culm Valley. Ellis was a director of the Bristol & Exeter Railway and a strong advocate for railways generally. He later claimed to own shares in most of the railways in the United Kingdom but was realistic enough to acknowledge that many expensive branch lines were more than some districts justified. Pain's original idea was along the lines of a steam tramway, without stations but with trains stopping as required at road crossings. The cost was estimated at £3,000 per mile and Ellis was sufficiently impressed to introduce Pain and his ideas to other people. One suspects these may have been members of the Exeter Chamber of Commerce in view of later connections with the CVLR (they shared an office in Exeter, for example). Pain certainly discussed light railways with the Chamber.

He envisaged a system of light railways radiating from market towns serving villages and farms, quarries and mills, filling the gaps in the national rail system left by main lines and their branches. Simplicity was the keyword, with a single line of minimal earthworks and a single platform, a shelter and perhaps a simple goods shed or shelter at each road crossing. If traffic was insufficient for a steam locomotive then horse power would suffice. The convenience provided by such a network would enable farms, mills, quarries and other rural industries to achieve their full potential. Both the land and the mineral resources could be fully exploited with adequate transport to take away the produce. The corresponding increase in value, albeit projected, of land and industry, should assist raising capital for the railway. Seeking the cooperation and support of landowners, and encouraging them not to seek exorbitant prices and compensation for the land needed for the route of the railway, was an important factor in Pain's argument.

In giving examples of the cost of construction Pain's ideas ranged from a three feet gauge line over flat country costing but £1,000 per mile for construction to a £5,000 per mile standard gauge line through hilly country. He placed great emphasis on meeting local needs and circumstances, in planning, construction and subsequent working. Regarding gauge he was quite ambivalent, acknowledging the cost of transhipment where a break of gauge occurred but stating this not to be a major problem where traffic was light.

On 15 May 1872 a meeting was called at the

---

* The Westleigh limestone quarries were leased by a group headed by J. C. Wall, General Manager of the B&ER. First proposed in 1872, the three feet gauge tramway connecting them with the B&ER main line at Burlescombe was built by the main line company, and opened in 1875. Its two locomotives were built in the B&ER works at the same time as those of the CVLR. The tramway was converted to standard gauge in 1898 and ceased use in 1950.

Let the reader again turn to the map, and he will see that most small towns and villages are situated on or near rivers or streams. Let him pick out a district, and he will observe that there are a number of villages, larger or smaller, one after the other up the valley. They generally consist of a number of small houses or cottages, a few shops and public-houses, and a sprinkling of dwellings of the better class; perhaps also there may be a mill or a small factory attracted by the cheap labour. Between these villages are homesteads, large or small, dotted about. All up the valley is good pasture or meadow land; as the hills rise on either side the pasture land gives way to arable, and here and there may be seen a quarry, limekiln, or brickfield; if these are absent, so much the worse for the inhabitants. The dwellers in these villages rarely move abroad, because they have no means of cheap locomotion. Cottages and houses are expensive to build, because the cartage of materials costs so much. Coal is dear, land is left undrained, and is not well farmed, because rents are so low that the landlord won't do anything; and the tenant, having no opportunity of seeing what others are doing, is content if he can make both ends meet, and pay the rent six months after it is due. This is no exaggerated picture, but one that may be seen more or less all over the back parts of the country.

Now, lay down a single light line of railway, or a tramroad, following the course of the river or stream and the surface of the ground, running close to the farmsteads, and mills, quarries, limekilns, or brickfields, and with a siding into each for their own special use when they want to bring in or send away a truckload of coal, oil cake, lime, bricks, stone, draining-tiles, straw, hay, timber, bark, or the hundred and one things to be brought in or taken out. Construct at each village and hamlet, or indeed at the crossing of any turnpike or main road, a simple platform, with a small shed for shelter, and a goods shed for general merchandise. Run two or three times a day each way an engine and a passenger carriage for the conveyance of the inhabitants, and when the engine is not thus engaged let it be hauling trucks from point to point. If the traffic be very small, then substitute horse power for the engine. A line such as this gives the maximum amount of accommodation with the minimum amount of disadvantage, and enables the landowners to obtain a better rent for their land, and their tenants to pay it. The land is then thoroughly developed as far as improved communication is considered, and the value being increased, capital is invested in improvements.

To traders light railways and tramroads are of great advantage, enabling them to buy or sell, bring or send goods with certainty and dispatch, and at a cost which can be known to within a shilling. Fresh fields for industry are opened up; mills, that only ground so much corn as was required in the neighbourhood, open out and extend their business because the transit is cheap; factories are set going that have stood idle since steam was introduced, and new ones are started. If there is any mineral wealth, its development is made feasible.

Extracts from Arthur Pain's LIGHT RAILWAYS AND TRAMROADS *published in 1873, illustrating his original concept. Pain could have had the Culm Valley in mind when he wrote much of this.*

George Inn, Uffculme, by Richard Bowerman, a solicitor, of Lambscroft. Attendance was good – a report listed 25 names and probably more attended – and William Furze, owner of the local brewery took the chair. Arthur Pain was introduced and he described the proposals and the course of the line. The meeting liked what it heard and agreed to support the proposed railway. A committee was formed of seventeen local men.

Pain was evidently asked to proceed, for a month later at a meeting at the Ilminster Inn, Uffculme, on 19 June, he reported that he had prepared plans and a draft prospectus. Only two landowners opposed the route; George Coombes, of Mountstephen, and the Misses Wood. The latter were represented by Coombes, who owned Selgar's Mill, and it would appear from later actions that he opposed the railway to the very end of the independent company.

A meeting at the New Inn, at Hemyock, in July or August was called to decide the site of the terminus. Some preferred the suggested site at Millhayes, apparently 'in case of an extension to join the London & South Western Railway', but the majority preferred Culmbridge as it was at the junction of several roads and would be easier of access to a wider area.

In November Pain was able to report that he estimated the cost of building the railway would be less than £3,000 per mile. At a meeting later that month the committee learned that the two land owners objecting to the route of the line were still refusing their consent to it, thus forcing an application for an Act. The committee originally hoped to take advantage of the Act of 1864 which enabled railway pro-

NOTICE.

NOTICE.

CULME VALLEY
LIGHT RAILWAY.

ON
WEDNESDAY FORENOON, the 15th of MAY, 1872
A
MEETING

WILL BE HELD HERE TO CONSIDER THE PROJECTED SCHEME FOR
FORMING THE PROPOSED LINE.

Any Person who thinks favourably of it is respectfully invited to attend.

RICHD. BOWERMAN,

Dated May 10th, 1872. LAMBSCROFT, UFFCULME.

Notice of the first public meeting, held at the George Inn at Uffculme, to consider the proposals for a light railway.

moters to dispense with an Act of Parliament if all the landowners along the route approved of the acquisition of their land. After notices had been issued by the committee of their intention to apply for an Act the objectors withdrew their opposition, but it was decided to proceed anyway. One of the main advantages of an Act was the compulsory purchase powers it gave for the acquisition of land.

The November meeting, at Uffculme on the 18th, was a public meeting of some importance, for the first directors were elected, despite there being no Act to authorise their appointment. They were:

Henry Samuel Ellis	Exeter
Charles John Follett	Exeter
William Furze	Uffculme
Edward Lutley	Hemyock
Henry Aylmer Porter	Exeter
Henry Drew Thomas	Exeter

Charles Follett was Mayor of Exeter at the time, a solicitor and also a member of one of the leading landowning families in the valley. William Furze was the founder and owner of the brewery at Uffculme, while Edward Lutley was a farmer and landowner at Hemyock.

Also elected were the auditors; William Cotton, manager of the National Provincial Bank in Exeter, and John Cave New, a local landowner.

At this meeting it was

Resolved unanimously that in the opinion of this meeting the proposed light railway through the Culm Valley to Hemyock is a sound and substantial undertaking both locally and financially and one especially deserving the support of the agricultural and trading interests in the district and of the public generally and that this meeting pledges itself to advance the prosperity of the line by every means in its power.

Pain hoped that they would be celebrating the opening before a year had elapsed.

At a directors' meeting immediately afterwards (at the Commercial Hotel, Uffculme; the committee seemed intent on working their way around the hostelries of the district) Arthur Pain was appointed engineer and Fred Pollard was to be secretary. It was agreed that Pain should be paid 5% of the estimated cost of £22,500, that is to say he would receive £1,125, but in shares and not in cash. Pollard's salary was to be £50 per annum. A Mr Richards declined to be a director and William Barnes, an Exeter banker, was elected instead.

Pain had first approached the Bristol & Exeter Railway in October 1872, seeking cooperation and assistance, and it had been left to J. C. Wall, the General Manager, to investigate and report back. He must have been reasonably impressed with Pain and his ideas for at the end of November Pain was invited to attend a B&ER board meeting to explain his concept of a light railway. He was told that the B&ER board were prepared to enter into an agreement to work the proposed line but with a number of conditions. They required proper station accommodation, for passengers and for goods, with platforms, station buildings and goods sheds that would permit loading and unloading under cover. The road bridges under and adjacent to the turnpike (subsequently the A38, and now the B3181) were to be of stone or brick and not timber. Whilst the light weight rails of the permanent way were accepted, better quality timber sleepers were to be used with ballasting of no less a depth than 15 inches.

This agreed they proved to be most supportive. Not only did they agree to work the railway for 50% of the receipts, when built, and to allow a rebate of 5% on traffic passing onto their line but they also agreed to guarantee the interest on the debentures and contributed 100 guineas (£105) towards the preliminary expenses of the Parliamentary Bill. Such support was valuable indeed and many small railway companies must have envied the CVLR its good neighbour.

It was also agreed at this time that the B&ER might buy the completed railway; if doing so within five years of opening by paying a premium of 10% over the cost price, or within seven years 12½%. The cost, however, was not to exceed £30,000. It was interesting to note that in view of the earlier comment about joining with the LSWR, it was agreed not to extend the line without the agreement of the B&ER.

Reporting the November meeting the *Railway News* was very optimistic of the railway's potential. The estimated receipts were £10 per mile per week and 'the works are so simple that six months will suffice to construct the line'.

With this support behind them the committee of directors entered 1873 intent on raising finance and organising. £10,000 was said to be already subscribed and some landowners were willing to take the cost of their land in shares. Many of the subscribers were local people. William Furze initially took 250 shares, £2,500, quite a considerable sum, while most of his fellow directors made do with 25. Fox Bros. took 100 shares and Captain Follett, Charles' brother, took 50. These initial holdings were increased later as the pressure grew to raise capital.

An enthusiastic meeting at Hemyock, at the Star Inn on 6 January, pledged full support for the line. The Bishop of Exeter was unable to attend but sent a letter of apology and support. His delightful letter is worth quoting to illustrate the mood and feeling of the time:

I wish well to the Culm Vale *[sic]* Railway with all my heart. The small property belonging to my family in Culmstock will not, perhaps, be very greatly benefited by the new line, since it is situated at the other end of the parish, and is already as near the Burlescombe station as it will be to any of the proposed new stations. But I travel much and am compelled to do so — and it greatly adds to my convenience if such lines as the one now proposed are constructed to penetrate the parts of the diocese which railways have not yet reached. I have no doubt that the new line will be of great use. The valley is rich in produce and well peopled. Traffic will greatly increase in it — year after year there will be more passengers and more goods conveyed. I shall be very glad indeed if the example now to be set in the Culm Valley is followed largely in other parts of these two counties. Light cheap railways will confer a benefit wherever they are introduced. All classes are, in my judgement, the better for any improvement in the means of getting about. Both rich and poor are the better for seeing more of their fellow-countrymen, for getting easier from places where people do not happen to be wanted to where they do, for the introduction of new ideas, new faces, new methods, and new materials. Railways contribute to all this, and I rejoice at their increase. I will take twenty shares in the new line.

The meeting unanimously carried a resolution calling upon those in the district to support the railway and, according to the *Exeter Flying Post*, 'the bells rang merry peals throughout the day in anticipation of the new railway'.

A meeting at Tiverton the following month, rallying support, said there would be great benefit for the town as custom would be brought there instead of to Taunton, Wellington or Honiton. Pain was there, saying he would keep contracts small so as to keep them in the reach of local contractors. He also said the country needed a system of light railways running into every market town 'so as to keep the trade within the district'.

Parliamentary work was also necessary for, in order to obtain sanction as a light railway, there was a need to fly in the face of what the Board of Trade then thought essential for a railway, such as bridges not level crossings.

Seal of the Culm Valley Light Railway Company (redrawn).

The Act was relatively simple, authorising a capital of £25,000 in £10 shares and powers to borrow a further £8,000. The company were given five years to complete the railway, were authorised to cross five roads on the level and to make agreements with the B&ER. One important clause stated the

> Railway [is] to be constructed and worked as a light railway within the meaning of and subject to the provisions of the Regulation of Railways Act 1868 providing that . . . the rate of speed authorised [is] 20 instead of 25 miles per hour.

Colonel Yolland, one of the Board's Inspectors reported that the level crossings could be approved if the maximum speed was reduced to 16 m.p.h. and the gates were carefully sited.

On 15 May 1873 the Culm Valley Light Railway Act 1873 received the Royal Assent.

With their Parliamentary authority attained the way was now clear for the directors to demonstrate their optimism and enthusiasm and build the railway.

MAP OF PART OF DEVON SHEWING THE COURSE OF THE

CULM VALLEY LIGHT RAILWAY.

PROPOSED LINE SHOWN THUS

STATION

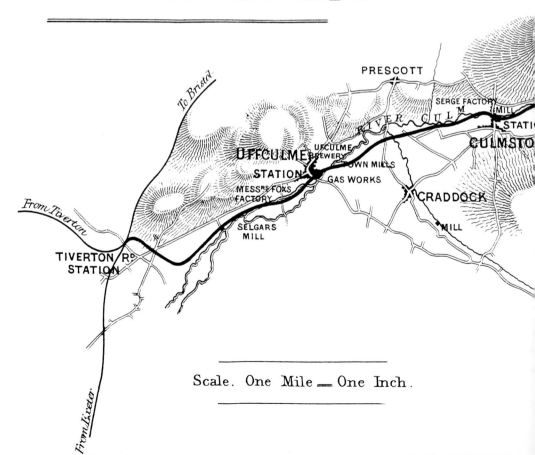

Scale. One Mile — One Inch.

CHAPTER TWO

CONSTRUCTION

'Large sums of money have been absolutely wasted on this line'.
C. J. FOLLETT, 1875.

A prospectus seeking subscriptions for the shares was issued on 25 September 1873. It stated that 1,400 of the 2,500 £10 shares had already been subscribed for and offered the remaining 1,100.

To encourage subscribers it advised that the line would serve about forty square miles and 6,610 people were claimed to live within reach of it.

> There can be no doubt, when the line is constructed, that a remunerative passenger traffic will arise while as regards goods traffic, the number of mills on the course of the line, into some of which sidings will be laid, the serge factories, and large brewery, the villages and farms it will run near or through, must ensure a considerable amount, consisting of Corn for grinding into flour, Hops and

Barley for brewing, unmanufactured Wool, household and steam Coal, Lime for building and agricultural purposes, artificial Manures, Slates, Tiles, Drains, Pipes, Brick, Stone, Cattle, and foreign Timber, going up the line; Beer, Woollen goods, Flour, Hay, Straw, road Metalling, English Timber, Bark, Cattle, Meat, Butter and Cheese, coming down the line.

It was estimated that the gross receipts from passengers and goods would be, at least, from £9 to £10 per mile per week. This was half what the Chard branch was taking and about two-thirds of the Cheddar Valley and West Somerset branches of the B&ER, so cannot be considered too extravagant a claim. The total cost of the railway was expected to be £22,500 plus a further £2,500 for parliamentary and

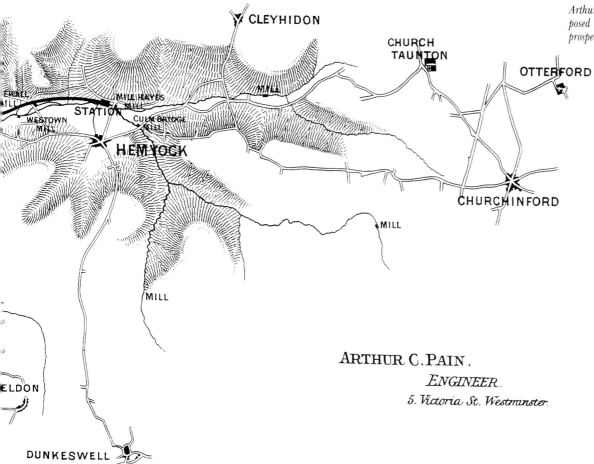

Arthur Pain's map of the proposed line that appeared in the prospectus promoting it.

professional costs.

The nature of the railway, as a light railway, was explained:

> As the name of the scheme implies, the Line will be constructed on a light scale – that is, the surface of the ground is followed nearly the whole way, whereby the necessity for expensive bridges, embankments, cuttings and other works will be avoided.
>
> In order to encourage this class of railway, so valuable to Landowners and the country generally, an Act of Parliament was passed, in the year 1868, whereby power was given to the Board of Trade to pass Light Railways for traffic, only limiting the weight of the engines used, and the rate of speed of the trains.
>
> The permanent way will, therefore, be much less costly than on ordinary Lines, because the weight of the Engines will not exceed Eight Tons on each pair of wheels, and the Trains will not be run at a greater speed than Sixteen Miles an hour. The Stations will be of the most simple and economical kind, and the few Bridges required, being small, will be constructed of Timber. The works being so unusually light, the Railway will be opened in about six months after it is commenced.

The prospectus concluded that '…it is nearly sure to prove a safe investment for capital at a rate of interest of between five and six per cent'.

The committee were now meeting regularly at Pollard's office at the City Chambers of the Exeter Chamber of Commerce but the first general meeting of shareholders was held at Godfrey's Railway Hotel, Tiverton Junction, on 2 October 1873 when the first directors were formally appointed by the shareholders. Fees of 200 guineas per annum, between them, were agreed. They were:

Henry S. Ellis
Charles Follett
William Furze
Edward Lutley
H. Aylmer Porter
William Barnes

Henry Ellis was Chairman and Charles Follett his deputy.

Ellis told the shareholders that their project was being watched with interest by eminent gentlemen and railway companies throughout the kingdom. Follett added that the line would be an example not only to the country but to the whole world. It had already been claimed that the CVLR was the first light railway in the United Kingdom but the directors were, alas, wrong in that claim.

One of the first railways authorised as a light railway under the 1868 Act appears to have been the Whitland & Taf Vale Railway, in west Wales, in 1869. It was opened as a mineral railway in 1874. In Devon the Barnstaple & Ilfracombe Railway had also been authorised under the Act in 1870 as had the Sidmouth Railway in 1871. It may well be that the CVLR was the first line to be built on firm light railway principles but it was by no means legally the first such railway.

Tenders had been sought in June, soon after the Act was passed, and an advertisement offered ten contracts:

The directors on the day of the official opening at Hemyock. Some of the local shareholders are no doubt amongst the crowd. Alas, individual names are not known although Pain is believed to be the younger person with side-burns and a cane.

COLLECTION M. J. MESSENGER

No. 1 Fencing. 21,648 yards run of larch, fir or wrought iron fencing, with gates, &c. complete.

No. 2 Earthwork. The earthwork and ballasting from the Tiverton Junction station to Selgar's Mill.

No. 3 Earthwork. The earthwork and ballasting from Selgar's Mill to Hemyock.

No. 4 Stone Bridges. Widening one under bridge and the construction of two over bridges.

No. 5 Timber bridges. Fifteen small timber bridges and 110 yards of tressill [sic] work.

No. 6 Timber station buildings. Three small passenger sheds, three small goods sheds and one engine house.

No. 7 Sleepers. 13,500 half-round larch, fir, or Dantzic [sic] pine creosoted sleepers.

No. 8 Rails. 488 tons of 40 lb rails, with fish plates and bolts, spikes and fang bolts complete.

No. 9 Platelaying. Laying 7½ miles of main line and sidings.

No. 10 Signal and telegraph. Six signals and 7½ miles of telegraph.

The shareholders were told that tenders were not being accepted until all the capital was subscribed but a week later Pain recommended accepting tenders from the following. The directors accepted his advice but not many were won by local contractors. D. A. Jardine, of Hawarden in North Wales, had the lion's share, gaining contracts numbered 2 to 5 and 9 for the bulk of the construction, for which he had tendered £6,893.5s.2d. Messrs O. F. & C. Varley, of Highbury, London, had the signalling contract (£208). The rails were to come from Crawshays of Merthyr Tydfil and their fastenings from the Patent Nut & Bolt Co. of London. Sleepers, too, came from a London firm, Burt Bolton & Co., as did the iron fencing, from E. Hernelewicz & Co. The nearest local contractors were I. H. Langdon, of Williton, who had that for the station buildings (£1,207.10s.5d.) and G. B. Sully of Bridgwater whose tender of £1,720.15s. for the wooden fencing was accepted. The total of the accepted tenders was £18,497.10s.7d. Apart from a Bristol firm, the only other tender from the south west was from Henry Turner of Wiveliscombe who unsuccessfully tendered for contracts 1 to 8.

The minute books for the following few months reveal little activity and one presumes the directors were taken up with practical legal matters such as the acquisition of land as well as raising money. However, in January 1874 Jardine was already asking for extra money.

Some 102 shareholders eventually contributed the total capital of £24,545 and a third of the amount came from the Culm Valley and its surrounds. Slightly more was subscribed from London and a sixth was from Exeter. William Furze was the largest shareholder with 510 shares, followed by the B&ER with 400, but even the people like George Babb, of the Star Inn at Hemyock, with just one share were important to the company. A full list of shareholders appears in Appendix 4.

The B&ER had agreed in October 1873, without their shareholders permission or the necessary parliamentary approval, to subscribe £4,000 by taking 400 shares. In return they had a representative on the Board of the CVLR and John Walrond Walrond, of Bradfield House, between Uffculme and Cullompton, took his seat in March 1874. Edward Lutley resigned to make way for him.

The B&ER were also preparing arrangements to work the line. Expecting it to be completed rapidly James Pearson, the B&ER locomotive superintendent, obtained his board's sanction to build two engines rather than try to acquire suitable ones from elsewhere. They were also seeking suitable carriages for the line and in March agreed that those on the Yeovil branch should be used, new carriages being ordered in replacement.

The spring of 1874 saw work start in earnest for in April Pain was able to report that between Uffculme and Hemyock the earthworks were in a forward state and that the contractor hoped to get the ballast down in a few weeks. Passenger and goods sheds at Uffculme were well in hand and were being roofed, while at Hemyock the foundations were being put in. Culmstock had not been started. There was little progress between Tiverton Junction and Uffculme as the company had only just agreed with landowners on land purchase. The rails had been rolled and were being delivered, and the first ship load of sleepers would soon arrive. The contractors, Pain said, had had no difficulty in obtaining labour.

In June Pain reported to the Board that the contractor had advised him that the railway would be completed before October. Such was Jardine's confidence that he asked for photographs to be taken of the local points of interest in order to decorate the stations.

The confidence proved to be misplaced, however, for in his September report Pain stated that the contract had not been pushed forward as rapidly as it ought. The Crossways cutting, a short distance out of Tiverton Junction, was proving difficult. 23,000 cubic yards had been excavated since March but a further 7,000 needed to be taken. The two brick bridges over the cutting were nearly finished. Only about 2½ miles of permanent way was laid but, apart from sleepers, the materials were to hand for the rest of the track. Jardine had opened a gravel pit at Craddock for ballast. Six of the timber bridges were complete as were the buildings at the three stations.

The Chairman, Henry Ellis, informed Jardine that they were not satisfied with the progress and warned him that if matters did not improve they would terminate his contract. Six weeks later, at the end of November, they had done so and Richard Broome was employed to finish the job on behalf of the company. Jardine was later described as 'not a man of capital, who squandered a great deal of time'. There was a little trouble getting him out but he went when he had been paid enough and Broome got on with the work. Pain's report of February 1875 was more optimistic, although he referred to time lost because of the very wet weather.

To help with the work a locomotive was hired, with driver, from Henry Hind & Son, of Nottingham. It was named *Lizzie* and arrived on 15 February 1875, but in an unsatisfactory state. After repair it started work on 20 February but broke down and was out of order from 17 to 30 March. Fox Walker & Co. of

Bristol sent replacement parts but on 10 April it again broke down and did not resume work until 30 April, after Fox Walker had sent a fitter. Hind & Son were charging £8 a week but the CVLR made substantial deductions from their bill to compensate for repairs and lost time. They also complained of the driver's 'incivility and direct disobedience'. Hind's only recorded comment is that new engines require constant repair, a strange remark. It has not proved possible yet to positively identify this locomotive.

On 24 April Broome was informed that, without expressing dissatisfaction with his efforts, the state of the company's finances would make them stop work unless the line was finished by 17 July. Broome's response to this deadline is not recorded but on 11 May the Directors, having heard the engineer's latest report, decided to open the line on 17 July. Until then they agreed they would visit the line weekly to keep track of progress.

On that same day, 11 May 1875, a Special General Meeting had been held to give approval to the parliamentary powers the B&ER were applying for, which would enable them to buy the CVLR in due course. Inevitably there were questions about the progress of the line and the Reverend Mr Edwards was particularly persistent. He pointed out that the public had been led to believe the line would be open in April and that he could see very little going on on the upper part of the line. Ellis assured him they were making every effort and Follett added about the weekly visits they planned.

The first weekly report of 14 May referred to a 'great pit' obstructing the line below Uffculme and which needed filling up. The permanent way below Uffculme was described as 'very shaky' and to add to the problems men were being lost to the militia.

Following the visit of 29 May a very long report was made by Follett, Barnes and Furze and this makes clear the lack of progress. Crossways cutting, at least, gave some good news for there had been considerable advance and the cutting was through but much work was needed clearing and sloping the sides, as well as raising and ballasting the line. There was no good news for the next section, to Uffculme:

> ...the most unsatisfactory part of the whole line, requiring the most diligent attention of the engineer and manager. Large sums of money have been absolutely wasted on this piece of line; work has to be redone. To the casual observer no progress appears to have been made, not a yard of actual progress has been made, the labour on this part of the line has been solely expended on perfecting raising and levelling the portion of the line hitherto supposed but erroneously supposed to be all but finished. Much to be done.

It was imperative that the ballasting was carried up to Uffculme so that the engine could get access to Culmstock to aid track laying beyond there. The pit still needed filling urgently.

The section from Uffculme to Culmstock gave the directors much more pleasure; 'progress has unquestionably been made'. The line was laid and ballasted to within a quarter mile of Culmstock but most of the gang were about to be removed to help with the lower section. Progress here was at the rate of a quarter mile per week. Although no track laying or ballasting had taken place above Culmstock, on the final section to Hemyock, they were confident that work would be rapid as it was straightforward and easy.

Back at Tiverton Junction work was about to start and this was considered most desirable 'so as to present the public and passers-by an appearance of business'. The lengthy and heartfelt report concludes

> The engineer is now by constant presence giving his unflagging attention and undoubted talents unreservedly to the company. The manager also doing all in his power. It is possible to carry the undertaking to a successful conclusion but it can only be done by a united and unflagging attention on the part of all concerned.

Finance to complete the line was such a pressing problem that it was offered as it stood to the B&ER but they declined to purchase it. A number of calls on shares remained outstanding, including William Furze, who owed £620 and Ellis, £100. To try to get some benefit from the summer traffic the directors would endeavour to get the line open to Uffculme and hoped the B&ER would work it.

The system of building the line by a manager – that is, Broome – was thought neither efficient nor cost effective and in June he was asked to tender to complete the line but he refused. His services were therefore dispensed with and the construction work was placed under the direct personal control of Pain from 19 June. A 'balance sheet' was sent to him to emphasise the seriousness of the financial position.

The directors were still aiming at an opening day of 17 July 1875 and in May had given notice to the Board of Trade. In July Pollard wrote to the Board:

> The directors are exceedingly anxious to obtain before the official inspection after completion an opinion of the Board as to certain new features adopted on the line. This is a railway of a rather exceptional character and constructed with a view to reduce the expenditure on lines in rural districts.

He admitted that this was an unusual request but said the directors sought assurance that they were progressing in the right direction.

The initial response from the Railway Department of the Board was to point out that as a light railway the CVLR must be worked subject to such conditions as the Board may make, but no arrangements had been made by the Board either as to construction or working. Such a pedantic reply, which did little more than paraphrase the relevant Act of Parliament, reflected not only the lack of proper legislation covering light railways but also a lack of willingness in the bureaucracy to help cater for them.

However a preliminary inspection was agreed and, after being put off for a month because things were not ready, Colonel Yolland reported on 14 July that the line was very much incomplete, particularly above Culmstock. He did not take exception to the permanent way and said the bridges were all substantially constructed and were standing well. The platforms at the three CVLR stations, however, were too short at only 74 feet while that at Tiverton Junction was too narrow and needed a shelter. Points into sidings needed interlocking with the signals and the sidings needed catch points. The sharp curves of less than 10 chains radii required check rails. Not all the level crossing gates were up but they should have lamps and crossbars and some telegraph poles and one of the level crossing cabins were too close to the track. The gate keepers huts, or cabins, at the level crossings, were a Board of Trade requirement that arose even before the inspection. They cost an extra £100 to provide.

The B&ER officer in attendance thought the platforms would take a six coach train but Yolland stated that that would call for platforms 140 feet long. He conceded

> in the uncertainty which exists as to what the amount of passenger traffic may be I think that if they are made 120 feet in length that may suffice.

He concluded that opening could not be sanctioned without danger to the public.

The hired engine had broken down again on 21 June and nearly two months were to pass before a replacement came. On 14 July the valley experienced the worst flooding in 14 years. During August there was a shortage of manpower, due to the needs of the harvest locally. Another problem arose that month when the Reverend Henry Bramley, vicar of Uffculme, started complaining to the Board of Trade and the company about the level crossing at Uffculme. Between a steep hill and the river bridge, the level crossing narrowed the road from 25 feet to 13 feet and the Reverend Bramley thought this dangerous and inconvenient. The Board referred the matter to the local authorities, and the company and the vicar eventually reached a compromise.

Tuesday 14 September gave the people of Culmstock some excitement when the ballast engine reached the village for the first time. Whilst this was taken as a hopeful sign the local newspapers also reported that there was much work to be done between there and Hemyock.

As was their wont, the navvies found other things to do than build railways, although to be fair those working on the Culm Valley seem not to have been as bad as some in the west country. A couple ran away for a month with two young married women from Uffculme. The townsfolk expressed their views on 5 November by burning not only effigies of the two women but of their husbands also, the latter for having the women back! A fortnight later it was reported the two women had left again, driven out by gossip. Despite this, Hemyock was waiting to welcome the navvies, not so much because their

presence meant the railway was getting closer, but because of the trade they would bring.

Another form of labour problem arose during November when the men working in the ballast quarry at Craddock went on strike. They were being paid 3s.10d. per day but Pain was trying to switch to piece work, no doubt to save money. Although many men were said to have left, Pain could not afford to compromise and was offering a reduction to 3s.4d. per day. The dispute was resolved apparently, for the following month a man named Jennings was almost buried by falling stones and earth in the quarry. He escaped with a bruised arm but was said to be accident prone.

As the end of 1875 approached, Pain was given an ultimatum to get the line open by the year end. Some dissatisfaction with Pain is indicated by the board's threat to call in a consulting engineer. Quite what were the problems holding up the line is not readily apparent, but there is a suggestion that the drainage of the Crossways cutting was not satisfactory. Pain hoped to have the line ready for inspection by the second week in January but this deadline, too, was passed. Pain was also working on other railway schemes at this time – the Swindon & Highworth Light Railway and the Southwold Railway – and was doubtless spending time in Wiltshire and Suffolk, away from Devon. Pain's relationships with the board were not always of the best once construction started. Back in May 1874 he had been told off for giving contracts without the board's consent and as the financial pressures grew so no doubt the board's tolerance diminished.

The directors were funding the increased costs of construction by an overdraft, having spent all the capital, and this was causing the company's bankers some concern, although the directors managed to hold out against their request for personal security until nearly the end of 1876. In August 1875 the shareholders had approved applying to the Board of Trade for a certificate to increase the capital by a further £7,000. It was decided to increase the application to £10,000 and the half-yearly meeting on 1 March 1876 approved this. Until the extra capital thus authorised was raised the overdraft, which was beyond the legal powers of the railway company, would not be reduced.

On 1 January 1876 the B&ER had been taken over by the GWR and the latter did not prove as benevolent a neighbour as the B&ER had been. The GWR directors were invited to look over the railway but had to be put off due to the now inevitable delays. Pain was told that if the line was not opened by 1 March the company would be out of funds. He responded positively that it should be ready. However, Colonel Yolland made a formal visit, in response to the company's request, on 12 February and listed a number of features that needed attending to. He suggested that the company should reapply when ready and the Board of Trade ordered the opening to be deferred a month.

To add to the directors' embarrassment at the slow progress the *Tiverton Gazette* ran a leading article asking pertinent questions.

> It is a common question nowadays to ask 'When will the Culm Vale Railway be finished', the answer is echoed back 'When?'. Time has gone on and here we are in the year 1876 with the line cut, rails down but the main point of carrying passengers and goods out of the question.

The editorial went on to express concern that the delays had increased the expense so that the line would never pay its way. They pointed out, correctly, that it was only the low initial cost of the proposed line that had given any hope of a return to its investors. A subsequent letter said that the shareholders were all interested in the agriculture or trade of the valley and town and would receive their profit indirectly.

It was suggested in February that a rearrangement at Tiverton Junction would save time and the need to purchase land. At first the GWR were unhelpful but later cooperated, although the work needed contributed to more delays.

Hind's engine broke down again in February and in March, and the GWR were approached to lend the locomotive that the B&ER had built for the line. This had been brought down to Taunton to be available for various inspection trains. Ellis found the hire charge of £3 a day, plus fuel and wages, somewhat expensive but had little option.

Pain, at the March meeting, reported that

the line was nearly completed with only half a mile of platelaying needed and three quarters of a mile of track, plus Hemyock station yard, to be ballasted.

According to Ellis, the GWR directors on their inspection thought the line had great potential for excursion traffic and urged Ellis to look at Cheddar, for example, where there was considerable weekend traffic from Bristol. They were anxious that the CVLR should cater adequately for similar traffic and suggested that if they did not the GWR would organise refreshment rooms and suchlike.

The line of the railway passed close to Selgar's Mill, between Willand and Uffculme, and a condition of the purchase of the land was that a siding would be laid in to the mill. A problem became apparent as construction trains began using the newly built line. The lane to the mill crossed the line on a severe curve and visibility was restricted. Henry John Brown, the miller, wrote to the Board of Trade to complain of the dangers:

> I feel assured if you saw the arrangement completed you would never allowed it to pass without a gate opener being placed there. As is now it is the most dangerous place I ever saw on any line. There are no small wicket gates for foot passengers. No signal that a person may know if a train is coming. No sound of a whistle to be heard for the noise of the water. No train to be seen until within sixty yards. And gate fasteners that require a man's power to open them. Either woman or child caught within the gates of that narrow trap if a train is coming will suffer death. It cannot be otherwise and I should never forgive myself that I had not pointed out the danger. There has been several narrow escapes already which causes me to write to you.

A Hemyock-bound train at the problematical occupation crossing at Selgar's Mill. The sharpness of the curve is readily apparent in this view from the train. The mill is to the right. 29 September 1956.

H. C. CASSERLEY

The Board were unable to do anything as the crossing was not a public road. Colonel Yolland noted the problem and suggested that when the siding was put in its signals could protect the crossing also. Meanwhile he advised that trains should approach at a very moderate speed, and whistle.

An accident that could have proved quite unpleasant happened in April. The foreman of the new school building at Hemyock had been 'taking refreshment' at Babb's New Inn, at Culmstock, and tried to jump on a passing train for a lift. He missed and fell between the platform and the engine but survived with a severe gash to the forehead.

Later that month the engine at last reached Hemyock.

On 20 May Colonel Yolland reinspected the railway and found much improvement. He noted that nameboards, lamps and clocks were still required at stations but agreed that the line could be opened to public traffic subject to certain undertakings.

The three undertakings he required were:
1. One engine only shall be in steam between Hemyock and Tiverton Junction.
2. The speed shall not exceed 15 m.p.h.
3. The weight of the engine shall not exceed 8 tons on each pair of wheels.

The GWR, as working company, duly gave the undertakings and, at last, the CVLR was ready to be opened. Far from taking the six months to build that the most optimistic commentator had suggested, or even the twelve months that Pain had forecast, the line had taken two and a half years in construction, and was still not complete. The cost, originally put at £22,500, was already over £40,000 and this was to give the directors a heavy burden for some years to come.

On the ground there were yet more problems. Whilst the directors and the Board of Trade may have been satisfied with the near complete railway the GWR was not. A dispute had been building up between the two companies as to the equipment to be installed at stations. The CVLR directors were surprised to learn that the GWR expected them to furnish the stations and evidently expected to hand the buildings over to the working company as little more than shells. In fact they could not afford to do much more. Now the line was ready to open the GWR passed on a long list of requirements to be agreed before they began working it.

The detail of the list says a great deal for the assiduousness of the GWR officers as well as for the standards expected by a main line railway company. It also echoed some of the points made by Colonel Yolland. Pain came to the defence of the railway and his work, arguing in particular that this was a light railway and ought not to be judged by the same standards as a main line railway, or even a branch line. The GWR were prepared to move but little and their list of requirements eventually returned to them with Pain's comments and observations noted on it.

He said the following had been done:
Buffer stop installed in engine shed, passenger platform at Hemyock fenced, padlocks put on level crossing gates, approach road at Hemyock ballasted, connecting signals at Hemyock.

He said the following would be completed as soon as possible:
Cranes in goods sheds, station nameboards, water closet apparatus, lamps at level crossings, water crane at Hemyock, lamps at platforms, in goods sheds and at level crossings, distant signals if required by the Board of Trade.

The GWR would provide the following but the CVLR had to pay for them:
Clocks at stations and in signal boxes, furniture 'as usually provided at similar stations', ticket cases, cupboards, shelves and desks and other appliances in goods sheds and offices.

Some things Pain considered unnecessary and objected to:
Cattle pens at each station, carriage docks at each station, yard cranes at each station, lamp room at Hemyock.

He also disputed other criticisms of the GWR and the argument rumbled on for a year or so. For the meantime, however, the agreement to the minor points satisfied the GWR and on Saturday 27 May 1876 a special train passed up the line 'depositing at the general stations stationmasters, clerks, porters and the necessary appliances for business.' The Culm Valley Light Railway was at last ready for opening to the public and on 29 May it did.

CHAPTER THREE
THE INDEPENDENT COMPANY

'This is a railway of a rather exceptional character'.
FRED POLLARD, 1875.

Thursday 1 June 1876 was set as the day for the formal opening of the line so the services that commenced on Monday 29 May should have passed without remark or fuss of any kind. However, that day coincided with the anniversary of some unnamed club in Culmstock and there, at least, the first train up the valley met with a fine welcome. Flags decorated the station and, with little apparent relevance, a banner reading 'The True Friends of Constitutional Liberty and Protestant Religion' was strung across the line. Several hundred people and the Holcombe Rogus Brass Band, playing the inevitable 'See the Conquering Hero Comes', were at the station and as the train left, to the sound of 'God Save the Queen', the cheers mingled with the peal of the church bells.

On Thursday came the official day of celebration in the Culm Valley and of particular rejoicing at Hemyock. The new Hemyock sta-

tion was decorated with flags and arches and the band of the Tiverton Volunteers lined up to meet the inaugural train. The vicar, the Rev. Popham, had chaired a committee, formed the previous November, to organise the celebrations and, by all accounts, they did well.

The train carrying the directors of the Culm Valley Light Railway arrived at half past one to be welcomed by the committee, the band and the first of many speeches. Ellis, in his response thanking them for the welcome, commented that to the directors it had been 'a work of much pleasure, and indeed a labour of love'. One cannot but wonder just how pleasurable it had been, as the problems of construction had dragged on.

The party immediately adjourned to a nearby marquee where three hundred people sat down to lunch. C. J. Follett presided in the absence of his cousin, Captain Follett, who was

A constable holds back the crowd for the official photographer at the official opening at Hemyock on 1 June 1876. Behind is one of the B&ER engines and the small carriages provided for the first services. The engine carries a flag on the smokebox and the bunting adorning the station is fluttering above the crowd. In front of the engine are the men of the Volunteers' band while behind the train is the very new timber goods shed.
COLLECTION M. J. MESSENGER

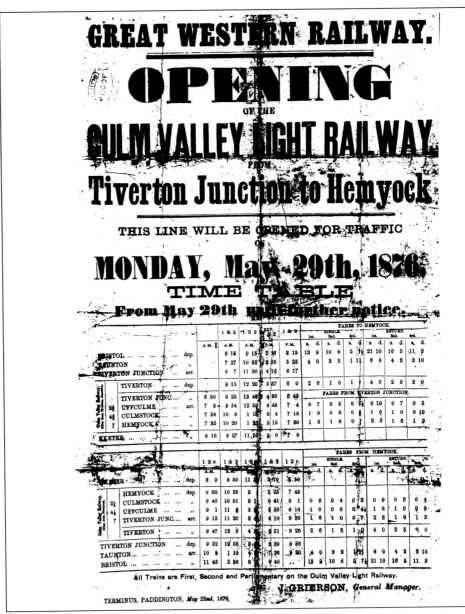

The announcement of the opening of the line and its first timetable, issued by the GWR.
TIVERTON MUSEUM

the largest local landowner, and most local people of some importance attended. The afternoon was taken with toasts and speeches and the feelings of the district were summed up by Follett's hope that the railway 'might be an incentive to agriculture and that it might improve the productive character of the valley.' He hoped it would

> bring forth the manufacturing powers of the valley, that it would give an additional impulse to the woollen trade and perhaps bring other trades and that it would be the means of taking away some of those superfluous flints in the place of which the parties taking them would leave in exchange some of their money.

Follett referred to the opportunities in the valley for sportsmen and hoped to see trains full of pleasure seekers looking for 'proper and decent accommodation' at the end of the line. He hoped to see there a grand hostelry called 'The Culm Valley Terminus Railway Inn'. There was great pleasure and pride that their railway was a pioneering light railway and the directors expected it to be an example to the rest of the country.

In the square at Hemyock some 250 'working people' sat down to a dinner provided by the committee. During the afternoon and evening there were 'rural sports and pastimes' in the field, where more refreshments were provided. The day was rounded off by fireworks and a ball in the lunch tent, Mr W. Metcalf's string band from Tiverton providing the music.

The GWR provided five mixed trains each way, with goods traffic being handled by the passenger trains. The initial timetable showed the first and last trains starting and finishing at Tiverton Junction suggesting that the engine shed at Hemyock was not ready for use and that the locomotive had to be stabled at Tiverton Junction. Certainly newspaper reports of the opening said that Hemyock was in an unfinished state. All trains took 45 minutes for the entire journey.

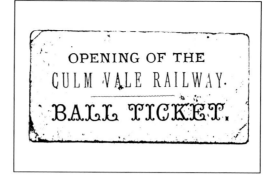

A ticket for the opening day ball at Hemyock.

The locomotives were those specifically built for the line by the B&ER. Numbered 114 and 115 by the B&ER, by the time the line opened

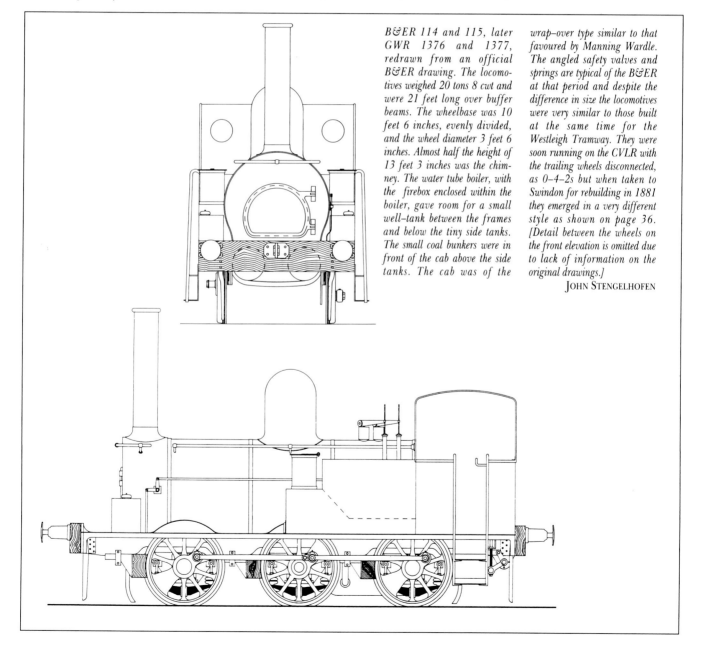

B&ER 114 and 115, later GWR 1376 and 1377, redrawn from an official B&ER drawing. The locomotives weighed 20 tons 8 cwt and were 21 feet long over buffer beams. The wheelbase was 10 feet 6 inches, evenly divided, and the wheel diameter 3 feet 6 inches. Almost half the height of 13 feet 3 inches was the chimney. The water tube boiler, with the firebox enclosed within the boiler, gave room for a small well-tank between the frames and below the tiny side tanks. The small coal bunkers were in front of the cab above the side tanks. The cab was of the wrap-over type similar to that favoured by Manning Wardle. The angled safety valves and springs are typical of the B&ER at that period and despite the difference in size the locomotives were very similar to those built at the same time for the Westleigh Tramway. They were soon running on the CVLR with the trailing wheels disconnected, as 0-4-2s but when taken to Swindon for rebuilding in 1881 they emerged in a very different style as shown on page 36. [Detail between the wheels on the front elevation is omitted due to lack of information on the original drawings.]

JOHN STENGELHOFEN

they carried GWR numbers 1376 and 1377. Both had been built in the B&ER works at Bristol, in September 1874 and December 1875 respectively, and were six wheeled coupled. They had 12 inch by 18 inch inside cylinders and 3 feet 6 inches diameter wheels. Unusually they had marine type boilers, an economy measure by the B&ER, and this left room for a well tank between the frames in additon to two small side tanks. In working order they weighed 20 tons 8 cwt, well within the weight limits for the branch. In view of the apparent urgency of their need Pearson, the B&ER locomotive engineer, had given their construction priority over other B&ER work. Joseph Armstrong, the GWR locomotive and carriage superintendent now responsible for the former B&ER lines, was not amused by the delays in bringing them into service.

The locomotive crews worked on two shifts. The early turn fireman prepared the engine in the morning and his late turn colleague disposed of it in the evenings. As this meant they, respectively, started and finished before and after their drivers the two drivers' shifts overlapped and the midday train was crewed by the two drivers. This practice continued until Hemyock shed closed.

It was in the permanent way that the light nature of the railway was most apparent. Flat bottomed rail of only 40 lbs per yard was used and this was bolted and spiked to half round sleepers of creosoted Baltic timber. A main line railway of this period would have been using 75/80lb rail. Rail lengths were 15 feet, 17 feet 6 inches and 21 feet. Ballast consisted of gravel and sand from the pit at Craddock and was barely one foot deep. Curves were as sharp as six chains (132 yards). The many small bridges, 31 in all, over streams and the River Culm were of timber although two overbridges, in the Crossways cutting, were of brick, as the B&ER had insisted. A third overbridge, between Tiverton Junction and the turnpike, was of timber also.

Soon after the opening Pain wrote to Bristol complaining that the locomotives were unnecessarily heavy for the line, obviously with his original concept of a light railway in mind, and stating that a locomotive weighing 12 tons would be ample and much more economical. He also noted that they were being driven at 25 or 30 m.p.h. and that the carriages were also heavier than necessary.

Understandably, as the older of the two engines was now nearly two years old, Armstrong was not impressed by such late criticism and pointed out that their axle load was

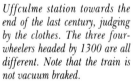

Uffculme station towards the end of the last century, judging by the clothes. The three four-wheelers headed by 1300 are all different. Note that the train is not vacuum braked.
R. J. SELLICK COLLECTION, NATIONAL RAILWAY MUSEUM

Monmouthshire Railways & Canal Company carriage in the guise of GWR No 1184, and lettered for use on the Culm Valley. Built in 1848 by Smith & Willey, of Liverpool, it came into GWR hands in 1875. It is recorded as being only 13 feet long and weighing but 5 tons. If the external condition mirrored its internal state it cannot have been pleasant travelling for its passengers. It appears to be standing on a length of mixed gauge track indicating a date prior to 1892.

COLLECTION R. C. RILEY

within the 8 tons specified, but he did agree to seek lighter carriages. The drivers had special orders as to speeds on the line. A derailment in July was noted in the minutes. Significantly in August, after a letter from the CVLR Secretary, Fred Pollard, Armstrong instructed the trailing wheels of the locomotives to be disconnected so that they became 0-4-2 and this was no doubt due to experience on the curves. All subsequent steam locomotives on the line were four coupled.

The GWR had provided small three and four compartment carriages from some unknown source, possibly the Yeovil branch as the B&ER intended. At a later date, possibly after Pain's complaint, they sent at least one built in 1848 that they had acquired from the Monmouthshire Railway & Canal Co. It was only 13 feet long and weighed but five tons. The three compartments shared one oil lamp.

Having achieved the opening of their railway the directors now had a changed scenario to manage. The GWR operated the line, staffed it and looked after its day to day running but new traffics had to be sought and improvements organised. The administration of the CVLR Company was also the directors' responsibility.

In July Cecil H. Newton was appointed

Assistant Secretary, on what seems a rather loose arrangement for payment, in that he would accept whatever the directors thought fit. Newton was already secretary to the Torbay & Brixham Railway (later Brixham branch) and the Buckfastleigh, Totnes & South Devon Railway (the Ashburton branch) and had experience of dealing with larger railway companies on behalf of small ones. Both his other two companies had been in dispute with the South Devon Railway.

It was already apparent from receipts that the GWR was not working out what was due to the CVLR in the most beneficial way. The smaller company was entitled to receive a proportion of the receipts from all traffic passing over the CVLR, calculated in proportion to the mileage travelled and, in the case of goods and minerals, an allowance was made for terminal costs. To complicate matters there was a rebate allowed on traffic passing onto the B&ER, SDR and GWR; effectively a commission on those railways' portion of the receipts. The GWR were clearly interpreting the agreements to their own benefit but to the detriment of the CVLR.

Half of the receipts were kept by the GWR for operating the line and the CVLR needed the remainder to meet their financial commitments, particularly interest on borrowed money. Although the estimated cost had been but £22,500 the actual construction cost had been twice as much, some £46,000, and, in the eyes of the GWR, the railway was still not finished. To fund the difference the directors had borrowed on overdraft against their personal guarantees. That the line, at a little over £6,000 a mile, had still been constructed remarkably cheaply was little comfort when the bank was pressing for news of repayment and there was insufficient income even to meet the interest.

Far from making £9 or £10 a mile per week, as the prospectus had forecast, the line was taking little more than £4. Total receipts for the seven working months of 1876 were £1,015 and expenses £609. This left enough to meet the interest due on the debentures, £360 a year, but little for the overdraft interest, about £600 a year, and nothing at all for the ordinary shareholders, who had been promised five or six per cent on their investment. Had the line been built within the estimate the shareholders could have received about three per cent; if the debentures had been the only debt they could still have been paid one or two per cent.

A special meeting of shareholders in 1875 had approved a draft application to the Board of Trade to raise further capital but this was not proceeded with. A later meeting, in October 1876, authorised the creation of £10,000 preference stock and a further £3,000 in mortgage debentures. Alas, the only additional funds this raised was £20 from Edward Lutley and £150 from Arthur Pain's brother in Liverpool.

New traffic was sought. The company had an obligation to provide sidings at Selgar's Mill and at Fox's mill at Coldharbour. Mr Lutley, who farmed at Whitehall, was also anxious to have a station there, not just for goods but for passengers also. There were also developments near Hemyock that might bring in additional traffic. At Uffculme a quarterly cattle market was started to generate traffic, but that called for the cattle pens that only a few months before Pain had thought unnecessary.

At Selgar's Mill the proposed siding would have cost £155 but to get it to the mill George Coombes, the mill owner, would have had to extend it across the mill pond at his own expense. An alternative line that would have cost the CVLR less was suggested but there was little or no response from Coombes and the subject lay dormant to become a problem at a later date.

Coldharbour Mill had been bought by Fox Bros. in 1797 to supplement their woollen mill at Wellington. The mill, formerly a grist mill

A view of Fox's mill at Uffculme, before the halt was built. The timber fencing between the branch and the siding, with a small hut, may have been the back of coal stacks. On the far right is one of George Small's private owner coal wagons.

COLLECTION M. J. MESSENGER

which was sited to take full benefit of the waters of the Culm, was converted to produce serge and worsted. A steam engine had been installed in 1865 to supplement the water wheel and coal for this was potential traffic for a siding. So would be the products of the mill, although a horse and cart continued to run regularly between the Uffculme and Wellington mills long after the railway opened. The Foxes were a Quaker family and particularly benevolent employers. Thomas Fox subscribed £2,000 to the railway in buying ordinary shares.

The Coldharbour siding was for the use of Fox Bros. and of the public and, after considering a loop, a simple siding was put in. It was complete by May 1877 and approved in June for opening after inspection by Major General Hutchinson. The delay had been due to difficulty in the supply of interlocking equipment for the pointwork. The signals there had been paid for by Fox Bros.

Whitehall siding was installed and opened with the rest of the line in May 1876. Lutley provided the land for it – it was adjacent to his farm – and there was some adverse comment at the half yearly meeting in March 1876. Some shareholders had gained the impression, from Lutley himself, that it was for his exclusive use. Pain dispelled this, stating it was always intended to be a public siding.

A little to the east, between Whitehall and Hemyock, the Folletts were attempting to exploit a deposit of clay on their lands with the aid of the railway. In September 1876 R. W. W. Follett and C. J. Follett had formed a partnership trading as the Culm Davy Brickworks. A siding from the CVLR was a priority, for getting plant in as well as the finished product away. Pain drew up the plans and the GWR, inevitably, objected to them. This did not stop him starting work and a compromise enabled the siding to be inspected and approved at the same time as Coldharbour siding. Culm Davy siding was paid for by the Folletts, who were to be permitted a rebate on their traffic to recover the cost. When it opened five minutes was added to the timing of one down train to give time to shunt the siding. At the brickworks a kiln was built together with an engine house, for supplying power for machinery, and a dry-

ing shed. The first order was received, with delight by C. J. Follett, in May 1877 but not until September was the first firing complete. The results were described as 'rough'.

On 3 January 1877 very heavy rainfall caused considerable flooding. Some distance east of Uffculme station the railway embankments formed a dam until the floodwaters reached the top, when about 20 feet of ballast was washed out. The next train passed over successfully, although the fireman was thrown off the footplate into the water, but traffic then stopped for the afternoon. The damage was repaired in time for the evening train and a couple of weeks later Pain put a culvert through the embankment to prevent a repetition.

Pain took the opportunity to point out how well the railway and its works had stood up to the very heavy weather and flooding. There was no damage and the station buildings had leaked but little. The GWR was not so satisfied and a whole new list of faults was drawn up in May.

340 rails showed defects with 200 needing prompt replacements. They were quite sure that 40 lbs rail was too light. Signals, level crossing gates, fencing, ditching, earth closets, the lack of lamp rooms and coal stores all came in for criticism, as did Pain's new culvert. Cattle pens were still required as were carriage sheds. The steps of some of the carriages were hitting the platform at Culmstock but Pain slewed the track to clear this.

At Uffculme some surplus land was exchanged with the parish for a piece between the bridge end and the goods yard, formerly the approach to the ford. This enabled the siding to be extended and cattle pens erected.

The arguments with the GWR dragged on for most of 1877, if only because the CVLR did not have the money to complete the work anyway. Much was made of the fact that the line was only constructed as a light railway, for which the works were adequate. The B&ER had approved the plans in the first place and the Board of Trade had approved the completed line. It was hardly the fault of the CVLR that the B&ER had been taken over by the GWR but all arguments failed; the GWR were not to be moved. Light railway theories were not relevant to them for they had their vision of what a railway should look like and that was what they wanted. Until agreement was reached the GWR would not take over the line fully, but merely operate it, leaving the CVLR to maintain it at their own expense. In June, in an attempt to pressurise the GWR, Pain was instructed to give notice that the CVLR would withdraw their maintenance team and leave such matters to the GWR. Whether he did is not recorded, nor is any response from the GWR who could, of course, simply have ceased operating the railway. By the end of the year it was agreed that the CVLR would undertake certain works, pay the GWR £300 to do others and the GWR would waive a few minor points, such as the replacement of earth closets.

Late in 1876 Lutley had suggested a passenger station at Whitehall, offering not only to give the land but to pay for the platform. It was hoped, rather optimistically, that by only putting down passengers they could avoid a Board of Trade inspection. Little more seems to have been done until the following June when the idea was combined with the aim of catering for excursionists. Lutley offered land not only for a station but for a 'shed' for day-trippers. A Mr Withers of Exeter was anxious to become involved but thought an hotel was essential, of which he would willingly become its tenant. Pain was instructed to prepare drawings and the Board of Trade were asked if, in order to catch the current season, they would sanction a temporary platform for setting down passengers only. Their response is not recorded, nor is any from the GWR. Lutley was offering £50 towards the cost of the station and Follett offered to match this but the whole idea was quickly put to one side in July.

Richard Hine of Hemyock wrote on 16 July stating his intention to erect a refreshment room adjacent to Hemyock station and a few days later produced a drawing of a building 55 feet long by 17 feet wide to seat 120 to 130 people. As well as the refreshment room itself it included ladies and gentlemen's retiring rooms, a parcels office and lavatories. After a site meeting it was agreed to build a footbridge from the east end of the station into the field. The CVLR would pay £40 towards this and the bridge

would become the company's property. Plans of the bridge were submitted to the GWR and there the matter rested for a few months.

The argument with the GWR over traffic receipts, terminal costs and rebates continued with little success. Counsel's opinion was sought and the advice was that the smaller company was being wronged and had a good case. The GWR refused to go to arbitration however.

Newton sought to increase 3rd class fares from 1d. per mile to $1\frac{1}{4}$d. per mile, except for the one statutory parliamentary train per day. Four months later, with characteristic belligerence, the GWR replied that they had no 3rd class trains west of Bristol and did not want them on the Culm Valley. By September they had agreed to the increase.

Pollard was dispensed with as secretary in June 1877 and Newton appointed in his place as the directors felt they had no need for two secretaries but needed one with traffic management experience. Newton's salary was fixed at £60 per annum and Pollard paid 50 guineas in compensation. They continued using his room at Exeter, paying £15 rent a year for that.

In June the pressure from the company's bankers, Dunsford & Co. of Tiverton, became too great and when they increased the interest rate the £16,000 overdraft was transferred to Mr Cotton's bank in Exeter. The directors had given their personal guarantees to Dunsford & Co. in October 1876 and they gave the same to the National Provincial Bank in Exeter. This meant, of course, that they were each fully and personally liable for the debts of the company.

Pain was giving problems also, the directors recording their surprise at the discourteous tone of his letters. He was claiming monies for extra work which was disputed. Eventually he was paid some cash and given a small number of shares in payment.

After the first full year of operations, 1877, it was clear that the small receipts were insufficient to meet the interest payments on the overdraft as well as the other commitments. Fortunately the GWR had taken over responsibility for guaranteeing the debenture interest when they took over the B&ER but the lack of sufficient income to meet their obligations troubled the directors greatly. In February 1878

An early view of Hemyock station with the erstwhile refreshment room behind. The three-compartment carriage stock can be seen on the siding behind the station, left. The gate in the foreground gave access to the river bank.

LENS OF SUTTON

they asked the GWR if they wished to buy the line but got a flat refusal from Grierson, the GWR General Manager, who said they were 'not desirous of purchasing any more lines or incurring additional obligations at present'.

The half-yearly report to shareholders, given in March 1878, did its best to be optimistic, pointing out the extensions of the Culm Davy brickworks and of Fox Bros' factory. Not only bricks but flints also, for roadmaking, were being sent from Whitehall where Mr Lutley had installed water driven crushing machinery. The refreshment rooms at Hemyock were nearing completion to cater for the coming season. Large numbers of 'pleasure seekers' passed over the line in the previous year and it was hoped that the new facility would encourage more. Improvements to the station facilities agreed with the GWR would stop traffic being lost to the LSWR at Honiton. The directors did regret that the Post Office were still not using the railway for mail, but continued sending a mail cart by road from Wellington.

Newton complained to the GWR in March of the slow speed of the trains. T. W. Walton, then divisional superintendent of the GWR, agreed trains were slow and commented 'I only wish the Culm Valley Company have made a road on which it would have been safe to run at the ordinary rate of speed.' He added that 91% of trains were punctual and that all goods traffic could be adequately handled by passenger trains. Removing the goods traffic to a separate train might speed the passenger trains but a passenger train would have to be taken off to make way for it.

The company received a severe setback on 13 May 1878 when Henry Ellis died. He had been involved with the project from its inception and brought a considerable knowledge of railway affairs to it. At the time of his death he was director of five other small railway companies, including the Torbay & Brixham and the Seaton & Beer, although he had ceased to be a director of the B&ER when that company was taken over by the GWR.

C. J. Follett succeeded him as chairman and William Furze became deputy. William Cotton, manager of the National Provincial Bank in Exeter, also a shareholder and an auditor of the CVLR, promptly stopped the overdraft, quite correctly, and months were spent in sorting out a new guarantee and whether Ellis's liability ceased on his death. In the event a new guarantee, for £16,000 was given jointly by Follett, Barnes, Furze and Porter, also Sir John Walrond and Mrs Ellis.

The directors must have found the ensuing months rather depressing for setback followed setback. The GWR refused to lend £3,000. Richard Hine objected to the footbridge at Hemyock and as the GWR refused to modify the plans to suit him the whole matter lapsed. Whilst the refreshment rooms had opened the

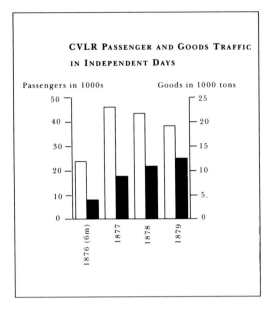

**CVLR PASSENGER AND GOODS TRAFFIC
IN INDEPENDENT DAYS**

Passengers in 1000s   Goods in 1000 tons

high of 46,000 in 1877, was steadily decreasing. In December Culmstock station became a telegraph office, to receive and send telegrams, although the Post Office would still not go so far as to trust the mails to the railway.

January 1879 saw the GWR threatening to cut out the last trains in each direction. The original timetable, and that which succeeded it following the transfer of the start and finish of trains to Hemyock instead of Tiverton Junction, had an early morning train, but at some time this was taken off and a late evening train substituted. Walton had done a count of passengers which showed clearly the low number using the last trains and the GWR had their way, although the directors sent a message hoping that they could be restored in the summer timetables. Their hope was in vain for the Hemyock branch had but four trains a day for the next forty years.

expected day trippers did not materialise and it did not last long. Newton got a job in London but at least remained as Secretary, although the company's registered office was moved to 1 Drapers Gardens in the City of London to suit him. Pain's services were formally dispensed with as the GWR had assumed full responsibility for maintenance of the line.

Some good news came in August when agreement was at last reached with the GWR regarding coal and coke terminal costs. The increased rates were backdated to the opening of the line, giving a modest boost to income. Goods and parcels traffic was steadily increasing, although passenger traffic, from an initial

Walton's passenger census counted passengers of all classes leaving Hemyock and arriving at Tiverton Junction, and vice versa:

TRAIN	DEPART HEMYOCK	ARRIVE TIVERTON JUNCTION	TRAIN	DEPART TIVERTON JUNCTION	ARRIVE HEMYOCK
8.30	5	20	9.30	6	5
10.30	4	16	12.50	12	4
2.50	5	10	4.25	13	5
5.20	3	7	6.30	11	5
8.20	3	5	9.25	6	2

Culmstock in early days looking across G. Dunn's coal yard. The cattle dock, left, looks particularly new but as there is a telegraph line to the station the photograph was taken after 1878. Already the station garden is beginning to flower. Culmstock Mill is in the background.

COLLECTION M. J. MESSENGER

By now the directors had had enough. Although Cotton, the bank manager, was clearly trying to be as kind to the company as possible, the weight of the debt bore heavily. Despite the depression the country was then in both traffic and receipts were increasing, although only slowly and the railway was still not achieving receipts of even £5 per mile per week. In 1878 the receipts from all traffic were £1,716 and expenses £915; the surplus was still not enough to meet both the debenture interest and that due on the overdraft.

Follett and Porter were instructed to take steps to dispose of the railway. Follett wrote at length to Sir Daniel Gooch, chairman of the GWR, setting out the position he and his fellow directors found themselves in and how they had a substantial personal liability which they had little hope to repay. An encouraging response had Follett explaining that they needed ready money to clear their debts. He suggested converting the £8,000 of debentures held by the GWR into preference stock, at a higher rate of interest. The company could then have reissued the debentures elsewhere along with the £3,000 of unissued debentures to raise £11,000. He also suggested the GWR should continue to guarantee the debenture interest.

This would have weakened the GWR's position considerably; whilst the debentures were secured against the assets of the railway, the preference stock would not have been, only being preferred over the ordinary stock. The interest would only have become payable if there was sufficient cash available. Thus the GWR would have had neither security of the capital sum nor the interest and, by guaranteeing the debenture interest due to some other party, would have had greater expense. Follett, Porter and Newton met Gooch, Grierson and Saunders, the GWR secretary, on 11 March 1879 and Gooch promised to put the suggestion to his board. Not surprisingly the board declined to assist.

Newton had already prepared a report considering the value of the railway to the GWR. He thought, optimistically, the Culm Valley line could give the GWR a shorter and quicker alternative route to London, via Ilminster,

Yeovil, Woodborough (in the Stert valley of Wiltshire) and Reading. It would avoid the Whiteball tunnel, between Tiverton Junction and Taunton, and would help keep the LSWR from the district. The GWR and LSWR were, as usual, in intense rivalry at the time with the latter reaching Exeter in four hours, over their shorter route from London; 25 minutes less than the GWR. Newton was hard pushed to find reasons for the LSWR to buy their line and only came up with the negative view that if it was extended to Chard it would stop the GWR building their short route. The idea of the GWR rebuilding the CVLR to main line standard was quite ludicrous and demonstrates either a lack of real understanding or the state of desperation that the directors were reduced to. The effort would have been as much as to start from scratch, as indeed the GWR did some twenty years later with their direct line through Somerton and the Stert valley. The gradients of an extended CVLR over the Blackdowns would have been extreme and it is significant that no railway was ever seriously proposed over this route.

Follett decided it was pointless offering the line to the LSWR, which he expected to be even less helpful than the GWR, and in July offered it to John W. Batten, a Parliamentary Agent with offices in the Temple, London, for £33,000. Two months later it was reported that Batten's 'friends' declined to purchase the line or lend money for it. The directors returned to Mr Cotton seeking to increase the overdraft to £18,000 and at the same time secured an overdraft of £1,000 from Mr Sanders at the Exeter Bank, again on their personal security. Newton now suggested that the company should apply to the Court of Chancery for a Scheme of Arrangement between itself and its creditors. This was effectively a form of receivership and a formal application was prepared.

At the same time Follett was in touch with Gooch again:

> We have now come to the conclusion that we must, even at a great sacrifice of share capital, dispose of the line. The board would do this with reluctance as they feel sure that a line which even through the present depression is not only holding its own but steadily progressing must be of sound value in time.

He asked informally if it was any use to approach the GWR again with an offer to sell, adding that they would accept £33,000. He posed the question 'Must we look elsewhere?' but Gooch is unlikely to have been moved by such a thinly veiled threat. Gooch did seek further information and was told how the sum Follett mentioned would repay the debentures and overdrafts in full and leave sufficient for the ordinary shareholders to get back 25% of their investment.

Whilst Sir Daniel may have given an impression of sympathy and helpfulness the subsequent dealings with F. G. Saunders were much more to the point and hardnosed. He condescendingly advised that the board did not wish to increase their liabilities but as the CVLR was not a very large undertaking they would try to help. The impression he gave was of one giving a favour although the eventual offer, worth but £25,500, was hardly benevolent.

This would have left nothing for the ordinary shareholders but after a further anguished letter Follett persuaded the GWR to give £5 for each £100 of CVLR ordinary stock. Follett clearly felt that Saunders and the GWR were taking advantage of the situation, and he was probably right. It was strongly felt that the GWR was not taking into account the potential of the line. Goods traffic was certainly increasing but the GWR claimed they were already losing money just operating the line. But as was

said later, when one party has no desire to buy and the other party is desperate to sell then negotiation becomes mere posturing. Certainly the CVLR were in a very weak negotiating position and could do little but formally accept the offer on 20 November 1879.

Not until 2 April 1880 was an extra-ordinary general meeting of shareholders held to seek their approval to the agreement with the GWR. Follett repeated the same points – that they had little choice. There was some dissent, however. Pain felt that the ordinary shareholders did not understand what was happening and sought to delay a decision for a month, being joined in this by Edward Lutley and Mr Farrant. Follett made the point that if the shareholders did not like the terms they could guarantee the overdraft themselves. No doubt there were more arguments but they are not recorded. The amendment was rejected and the motion to sign the agreement was approved. On 5 August 1880 the common seal of the GWR was affixed to the agreement.

Having reached a decision the final tidying up of the company's affairs remained. Pain was brought in to report that all had been done that the company was obliged to do or that the GWR demanded. He was paid three guineas for his report which stated that only the siding at Selgar's Mill remained outstanding. After unsuccessfully trying to pay Mr Coombes £50 in compensation formal negotiations began. The GWR engineer had told Coombes' solicitor

Uffculme station photographed by local decorator and photographer G. Crease. The locomotive is clearly a saddle tank and may well be from the Whitland & Taf Vale Railway (see Chapter 4), in which case the date is about the 1890s. A semaphore signal can be seen to the left.

COLLECTION M. J. MESSENGER

that the siding would cost £600 to construct and he therefore sought £300 in compensation. The CVLR directors believed it could be built for £250 and offered £200, resolving to build the siding themselves if Coombes refused. In the end he said he would take £250 and settlement was reached.

Other small details bothered the directors at this time. Since 1877 there had been talk of lighting Uffculme station with gas from the local works, at a cost of £12 for fittings. The CVLR agreed to pay half this. By 1880 the work had been done but the GWR refused to pay the other half. The CVLR therefore declined to pay their £6, saying they could not afford it anyway, and John Thorn, manager of the Uffculme Gas Company, was left to take them to court.

There was also a dispute of some sort over the ballast field at Craddock. It appears to be something to do with the nature of gravel taken and the condition the field was left in. At one point the minutes note that more had been paid in rent than it would have cost to buy the freehold of the field, and the argument fizzled out.

Fox Bros. had wanted the river bank at Uffculme repaired and after pointing out that the company had no money to pay for this it was agreed to transfer to them a strip of land in compensation and to release the CVLR from their obligation to repair the river banks.

In February 1881 a payment of 3% was made to the ordinary shareholders, with the exception of the GWR and some others who were not fully paid up. Although described as a dividend it was, in fact, a capital distribution.

The meeting of 19 May 1881 was held at the offices of the London Tilbury & Southend Railway, at Fenchurch Street, London, as Newton had been appointed secretary of that railway company. He resigned as CVLR secretary but agreed to assist the remaining business of the company. He was paid an honorarium of £50 although the next minute stated they could not afford to pay the auditors.

In August, in an unusual display of magnanimity, the GWR agreed to forgo the dividend on their holding of 160 ordinary shares, £4,000 in value, (although it must be noted the dividend was being paid out of their money) and a final payment of $2^{1}/_{2}$% was made to the ordinary shareholders.

The final meeting was at Fenchurch Street on 3 November 1881 attended by Follett, Furze, Porter, Barnes and Newton. The debenture and preference stock had been repaid in full, the overdrafts repaid and the ordinary shareholders had received $5^{1}/_{2}$% of their original investment back, eleven shillings for each £10 invested.

Follett's final comments summed up the history of the railway:

> We have arrived at the final meeting of a company formed to promote a very small undertaking in the way of railway enterprise which was commenced in Devonshire in 1873. The main object was to ascertain if a light railway running through a not very thickly populated agricultural neighbourhood could be made remunerative. The district was not solely agricultural, because there was a moderate sized town possessing a large brewery and several considerable villages on the line of route. There was no doubt that the design as at first intended would have been successful but, as had happened in many other cases, the estimate put forth by the engineer unfortunately turned out to be less than the ultimate expenses entailed by almost one half. One cause that militated against them was the rise in the price of materials, the second was that the contractor who undertook the work failed and it had to be placed in the hands of another. In consequence of these misfortunes the line took three or four times the period contemplated in completing besides costing twice the money originally estimated. Receipts of traffic showed that if it had not been for those drawbacks the directors would have been able to declare fair dividends upon the amount expended. In consequence of the expenditure largely exceeding the amount fixed upon the directors were compelled to raise money to finish the undertaking, and as they saw no chance of making the line pay they were compelled to go to the Great Western Company and ask them to purchase it giving a very sorry return to the shareholders. The correspondence which passed between the two companies was not so agreeable as it might have been but in the end the directors of the Great Western met the shareholders in a fair and considerate manner.

He concluded his report:

> The duties of your directors are completed and as soon as the report and accounts now submitted have been passed by the shareholders the Culm Valley Light Railway Company will . . . be dissolved and cease to exist.

Tiverton Junction in 1924 before rebuilding. A GWR mogul passes through with an up train whilst the Culm Valley train waits on the left. The signal cabin for the branch line is to the right of the branch locomotive.

G. N. SOUTHERDEN,
COLLECTION M. J. MESSENGER

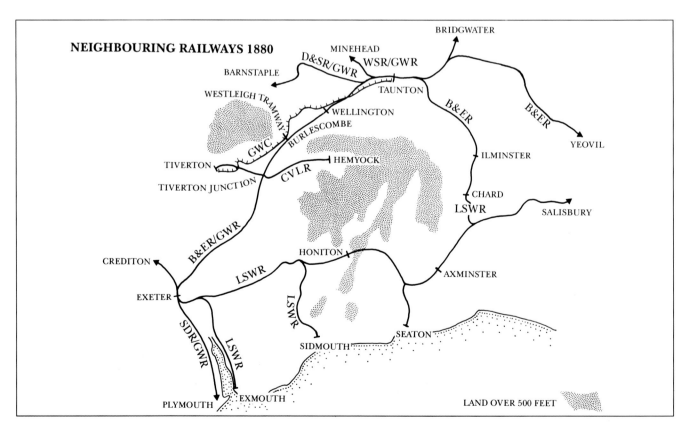

NEIGHBOURING RAILWAYS 1880

BRIDGWATER

MINEHEAD

D&SR/GWR   WSR/GWR

BARNSTAPLE

WESTLEIGH TRAMWAY

TAUNTON

B&ER

B&ER

WELLINGTON

YEOVIL

GWC.

BURLESCOMBE

TIVERTON

ILMINSTER

HEMYOCK

CVLR

TIVERTON JUNCTION

CHARD

LSWR

SALISBURY

B&ER/GWR

HONITON

CREDITON

AXMINSTER

EXETER

LSWR

LSWR

SDR/GWR

LSWR

SEATON

SIDMOUTH

PLYMOUTH   EXMOUTH

LAND OVER 500 FEET

CHAPTER FOUR
A GREAT WESTERN BRANCH

'Long may our society, modern as it is, find a place within its complex structure for rural, unhurried lines such as this'.
P. W. GENTRY, 1953.

Since early 1878, when the Great Western took over the maintenance of the Culm Valley Light Railway and thus full responsibility for it, the line had effectively been a branch of that system. From 5 August 1880 the line was totally a Great Western branch. Regrettably, little information survives from the latter part of the nineteenth century and certain detail can only be surmised.

One snippet from the GWR directors' board minutes is the decision in September 1880 to write off 6s.2d. stolen from Culmstock station on 5 May.

It would be reasonable to assume a continued and steady growth in goods traffic paralleled by a decline in passengers carried, for these trends were evident in the independent company's figures. The refreshment room at Hemyock did not last long but found a new use housing farm stock.

One source of goods traffic that did not prove fruitful was the brick works at Culm Davy. On 25 May 1880 the Culm Davy Brick & Tile Co. Ltd. was incorporated with, as shareholders, the two Follett cousins, William Bailey of Culm Davy brick works, Cecil Newton, A. U. Higgins, an architect of New Malden, two gentlemen from Exeter and Miss Nelly Follett of Surbiton. Newton was the company secretary. The company had leased the brick works from the Folletts and was not only to carry on the business but was also intended to obtain a contract to supply bricks for the Severn Tunnel, then under construction. William Moss, a contractor of Stafford who was building the Exe Valley Railway at the time, was also involved and may have had a further lease. Had the company gained the contract it would have become a valuable industry indeed to the Culm

A Culm Davy brick.

Valley and to the railway but, alas, it did not and neither it nor Moss paid the Folletts any rent. It was wound up in July 1881 and by the time the Ordnance Survey mappers reached the area in 1888 the brick works was disused and the siding and its connection to the branch removed.

GWR Bristol and Exeter Division service timetable (working timetable) October 1879.

CULM VALLEY BRANCH.

TIVERTON JUNCTION TO HEMYOCK.

Down Trains.   Narrow Guage.

Miles.	STATIONS.	1 Pass.	2 Pass.	3 Pass.	4 Pass.	5	6	7	8	9
		A.M.	P.M.	P.M.	P.M.					
	Tiverton Junction dep	9 25	12 50	4 25	6 25	...	...	...	...	...
	Cold Harbour Siding ... "	C.R.		...	...					
2¾	Uffculme ... ... "	9 49	1 9	4 44	6 44	...	...	...	...	...
4¼	Culmstock ... ... "	10 4	1 24	4 59	6 59	...	...	...	...	...
	Whitehall Siding ... ... "	C.R.		..	...					
6¾	Culm Davey Siding ... "		C.R.	..	...					
7¼	**Hemyock** ... ... arr	10 20	1 40	5 10	7 10	...	...	...	...	...

C.R.—Stop when required.

HEMYOCK TO TIVERTON JUNCTION.

Up Trains.

Miles.	STATIONS.	1 Pass.	2 Pass.	3 Pass.	4 Pass.	5	6	7	8	9
		A.M.	A.M.	P.M.	P.M.	...				
	Hemyock ... ... dep	8 30	10 30	2 35	5 20		...	...	...	...
	Culm Davey Siding ... "			...	...					
	Whitehall Siding ... ... "			..	...					
2¼	Culmstock ... ... "	8 46	10 46	2 51	5 36		...	...	...	...
3¾	Uffculme ... ... "	9 1	11 1	3 6	5 51		...	...	...	...
	Cold Harbour Siding ... "		C.R.		...					
7¼	**Tiverton Junction** arr	9 15	11 15	3 20	6 5		..	...	...	...

Single Line worked by Train Staff. The Train Staff Stations are Tiverton Jc. and Hemyock.

GWR 1376, originally B&ER No 114, at Oswestry on 31 May 1932, where it was allocated to work the Tanat Valley Light Railway. It had been rebuilt drastically in 1881 with a new boiler and longer wheelbase so by this time bore little resemblance to its original condition.

H. C. CASSERLEY

The GWR no doubt commenced a rolling programme of improving the permanent way and structures of the line. Replacing first the defective rails, they would soon have disposed of the 40 lb rail that they so disliked. It is interesting to note that the other Pain standard gauge railway under construction at this time, the Swindon & Highworth Light Railway, was lent money by the GWR, who were to work it when built, in order to have a more substantial type of permanent way. The timber bridges were steadily replaced with iron.

The two B&ER locomotives did not last long either. Both were taken to Swindon to be rebuilt with new boilers and longer wheelbase in September 1881 for use on the quay tramway at Weymouth. 1377 was withdrawn in 1927 whilst 1376 was then sent to Oswestry for a further seven years to work the Tanat Valley line.

To replace them came 1298 and 1300. These 2-4-0 side tanks had been intended to be broad gauge locomotives, having commenced building in 1875 at the South Devon Railway's Newton Abbot works, where they were allocated the names *Saturn* and *Mercury*. (The SDR did not number their engines.) When the SDR was

1300 on the siding between the station building and the old goods shed at Hemyock. Signs of its 1905 rebuilding are apparent when compared with the earlier photograph at Culmstock on page 24. Vacuum brakes have been added and the smokebox has been rebuilt to accommodate the feed water heater. The number plate has also been moved from the centre of the tank to the cab side.

H. C. CASSERLEY

taken over by the GWR work stopped and the unfinished locomotives were taken to Swindon to be completed in 1878 as standard gauge engines. They became regulars on the branch for many years.

Early in the morning of Tuesday 18 January 1881 such a vigourous snowstorm started that by the afternoon the line was blocked and trains ceasing running. Snow fell continuously for 36 hours, with more falls during Thursday and Friday. Culmstock was completely isolated and on Friday evening both the CVLR and the Tiverton branch were still blocked.

Ten years later came a repetition of such weather, only much worse, and this was to become known as the Great Blizzard. On Monday 9 March 1891 the snow started at about 2 p.m. and lasted until 2 a.m. on Wednesday morning; 36 hours as ten years before. The Culm Valley train could not run on Tuesday or for the rest of the week. As the *Tiverton Gazette* reported:

> The block on the Culm Valley branch was complete. The line was literally buried and to use an official's phraseology 'could not be found'.

The mail cart could not get through to Hemyock and Fox's factory also ceased work on Tuesday, but was able to recommence on Thursday as most of the employees lived close by. The GWR gangs, with their snowploughs, cleared the main line first but reached the Culm Valley on Friday.

A meeting between four Hemyock men in

1885 was to have profound effects for both Hemyock and the railway. John Clist, Samuel Farrant and Edward Lutley were farmers and joined with James Wide, a butter factor, to tackle the growing agricultural depression. The development of refrigeration during the 1870s enabled dairy products to be shipped half way around the world and still compete with home-grown products. As imports increased so prices fell, notably after 1883, and the labour intensive farmhouse manufacture of butter and cheese became less profitable. Another technological development, however, was that of the centrifugal separator, which enabled cream to be separated from milk mechanically and at great saving in time.

The result of the meeting was the founding

How the Great Blizzard of January 1891 stopped all rail traffic is readily apparent in this view of Uffculme. The stop signal at the level crossing appears to be in the 'off', or all clear, position but this must be either snow on the signal wire or sheer optimism.

COLLECTION M. J. MESSENGER

The entrance to the butter factory at Hemyock showing the two sidings that were in place by 1904. The trackwork is particularly light. Millhayes Mill was at the end of the sidings and to the left.

COLLECTION M. J. MESSENGER

BUTTER FACTORY
HEMYOCK. 11

the following year of the Culm Valley Dairy Company, a pioneer butter producer that was first established at Clist's farm at Mountshayne, just south of Hemyock. Milk was brought in from local farms to pass through a steam pow- ered separator and the resulting cream was churned into butter. The factory was one of the earliest mechanical butter manufactures in the country, and certainly in the west of England, producing a butter of consistency and quality that the farmers' wives could not previously achieve laboriously making it by hand. The but- ter was packed and despatched by rail all over Britain. All of the four men, or members of their families, had been shareholders in the CVLR so they were aware of the benefits trans- port could bring to an area. An essential part of the economic equation was the disposal of the skimmed milk by-product and piggeries were established for this purpose. A pig market was later started at Hemyock and provided addi- tional traffic for the railway.

To invest heavily at a time of depression and declining profits was an act of considerable courage but the venture was successful, aided by the transport services available from the

GWR. To ease the load at Mountshayne small depots were set up in the surrounding district. They received the milk, separated it and just the cream was sent on to Hemyock to be churned. The first such depot was opened at Culmstock in January 1888, in the former corn mill owned by Fox Bros. New milling machin- ery was also installed there to help provide feed for the Hemyock piggeries. A company was incorporated in 1888 by the four men, with a capital of £5,000, to continue the business, and all the shareholders were local Hemyock peo- ple. The first separation had taken place on 16 May 1886 and in that month 3,000 gallons of milk were handled. In the same months in the successive years the gallonage was 17,000, 36,000, 47,000 and, in 1890, over 100,000. More than 250 gallons of milk were needed to produce a hundred-weight of butter.

The trade continued to expand and was fast outgrowing Mountshayne. In the mid- 1890s the company bought the mill at Millhayes, which already had siding access across the road from Hemyock railway station. Milling continued, producing animal feed- stuffs, and a new butter and cheese factory

Probably in the early years of this century, 1300 at Hemyock with rather more substantial four-wheelers than were origi- nally used. All steam locomotives faced east, up the gradient, thus exposing the crews of open cab engines to the westerly winds on the return trips.

COLLECTION M. J. MESSENGER

built. The output of the factory, being perishable, was conveyed by passenger train and in 1903 Hemyock took nearly £1,200 in parcels traffic, more than five times the Uffculme figure.

In May 1888 the Upper Culm Valley Dairy Company, and Farmers' Association, Limited was founded, based at Bollhayes in Clayhidon, no doubt inspired by the enterprise at Hemyock but, alas, it was not so successful and unable to trade because of its debts was wound up in 1892.

When the railway was opened in 1876 both the CVLR and the GWR had to undertake to the Board of Trade that only one engine would be in steam between Tiverton Junction and Hemyock, that is to say that only one train could be on the line at any one time. At the same time the Board had insisted the line be worked on the Absolute Block system whereby it was divided into sections controlled by telegraphs at the stations at each end of the sections so that only one train could be in a section at the time. In the mid-1870s the Board of Trade's Railway Inspectorate were, quite rightly, concerned at the level of safety on railways, particularly single lines. They were rigorously insisting on the introduction of the block system throughout the British Isles but it does seem somewhat over-zealous when they already had an undertaking that the line would be worked on the one engine in steam principle.

The line was divided into three sections, Uffculme and Culmstock providing the divisions between the termini. The signalling was provided by a little known firm of contractors, O. & F. H. Varley, of Highbury, London, who also took two shares, but what equipment they installed is not recorded. Early plans suggest that disc and crossbar signals were in use as well as conventional semaphores. Pain was authorised to purchase Tyer's telegraphs in 1874 but it is not known if he did. Colonel Yolland refers to the interlocking of points and home signals being of an unusual kind, rather flimsy and needing adjustment. The Board had agreed that the line did not need distant signals although the level crossings had to be protected with stop signals. Some photographs taken at about the turn of the century show signal

posts at the level crossings carrying two arms, one for each direction.

In February 1902 the GWR wished to renew the signals and pointed out to the Board of Trade the anomaly of having the absolute block system when the line was worked by one engine in steam. They asked if they could waive the absolute block telegraph requirement. The Board agreed, even going so far as to say it was absurd and adding that no signals were necessary. The GWR gave a fresh undertaking that the line would be worked by one engine in steam carrying a staff, that the speed would not exceed 15 m.p.h. and that the engine would not exceed eight tons weight on each axle.

Traffic figures are available again for 1903 and we get a brief glimpse of how busy the branch was. Total passenger tickets issued was 18,838, half the number of 1879. Goods traffic

A charming study of children on the level crossing at Culmstock, by Gregory Crease. Of particular interest is the double arm signal on the station side of the gate, presumably the original installation.

COLLECTION M. J. MESSENGER

This view of GWR 1384 (ex-Watlington & Princes Risborough Railway No 2) shows the Pain designed timber engine and carriage sheds quite distinctly. Note the unusual doors on the engine shed and the large lump coal on the stage beneath the water tank. Note also the timber stays giving additional support to the carriage shed. Some of the track had been relaid in bull-head rail. 1384 is in very clean condition.

COLLECTION R. C. RILEY

was much the same at 12,132 tons, of which only 1,617 was despatched. More than a third of the goods received was coal. Uffculme was the busiest station for goods with Hemyock close behind but Culmstock a poor third. However Culmstock sold more tickets than Hemyock. In addition a wagon or two a week of livestock was handled at each station. There were four staff each at Uffculme and Culmstock and three at Hemyock. The total wages bill for 1903 was £513.

By 1913, the next figures available, the passenger figure had dropped slightly but goods traffic had doubled. This was due almost entirely to what the GWR described as 'other minerals' sent from Culmstock and Hemyock amounting to over 12,000 tons. A James Yates had set up about 1906 as a coal merchant and quarryman at Hemyock, quarrying stone from Coombe Hill, north of Hemyock station, and he was probably the cause of this. In 1911, with others, he incorporated the Hemyock Stone & Coal Company Limited to take over his business. By 1913 the company's registered office had moved to Hemyock station yard but in 1916 Yates appointed himself liquidator of the company. Other goods – coal, merchandise and parcels – were much the same as ten years before but livestock had increased. Although Culmstock had dropped back, Hemyock had

increased by 50 per cent and Uffculme had more than doubled. There were changes on the staff side. Uffculme had lost one man and Culmstock was controlled by Tiverton Junction and run by but one person. Hemyock had gained a man so there were now nine staff on the branch and the wages bill was little changed at £529.

Whilst 1298 and 1300, the two ex-SDR engines, were the mainstay of the line for more than forty years, a number of other interesting locomotives were also used, often briefly. One of the least recorded is the saddle tank locomotive that appears in a photograph of Uffculme station by Crease. There is little to identify the engine but it has been suggested that it was from the Whitland & Taf Vale Railway. That railway had become the Whitland & Cardigan Railway in 1877 and was worked by the GWR from 1886. Both its Nos 1 and 2 were small 0-6-0 saddle tanks of similar design. No 1 was rebuilt at Swindon in 1894 and then spent time in the west country before being sold out of service in 1912. No 2 was rebuilt in 1887 at Swindon and was also sent to the west country until being sold in 1911. Significantly No 1, as GWR 1385, is said to have worked as an 0-4-2 prior to rebuilding. However the photograph does not show the name plate *John Owen* it carried on the saddle tank but either locomotive could equally have been on the CVLR and be the one shown in the photograph.

Rather more is known of another visitor. 1384 had been built for the Watlington & Princes Risborough Railway in 1876, where it was their No 2, and was acquired by the GWR in 1883. It was used on the construction of the Bodmin branch in 1886, lent to the Lambourn Valley Railway in 1898 and used by the GWR itself on the Wrington Vale Light Railway (opened 1901) and the Culm Valley. The GWR withdrew it from service in 1911 and it ended up as No 4 *Hesperus* on the Weston, Clevedon & Portishead Railway until it was cut up in 1937. During March 1905, 1300 was at Swindon being rebuilt and providing relief is a likely reason for visitors to be at Hemyock shed.

In 1906 the GWR had acquired the Manchester & Milford Railway (despite the grandiose title this Welsh railway ran from Pencader Junction, north of Carmarthen, to Aberystwyth, and Henry Ellis had been a director briefly in the 1870s) and with it some rather small bogie carriages. Three soon found their way to the Culm Valley to replace the old four wheel stock and remained until the 1930s. Two, GWR numbers 7898 and 7899, were built in 1895 as tri-composites but for the CVLR were modified by having two compartments converted into a guards/luggage section, leaving two

GWR 1384 at Hemyock with the ex-Manchester & Milford carriages. The locomotive and carriages together mean the photograph was taken between 1906 and 1911. The hamper on the platform is lettered A. Wide.

COLLECTION M. J. MESSENGER

first class and three third class compartments. Both had short wheel-base bogies and their length was stated to be about 41 feet. They were demoted to brake thirds in 1927 and renumbered 657 and 606. The third carried GWR number 3982 and was a brake third, with three passenger compartments. Built in 1892 it was shorter than the other two, at about 37 feet, and its bogies also of short wheel-base. All must have improved the comfort of Culm Valley passengers.

Although established to meet foreign competition in agricultural products, as the Great War approached the Culm Valley Dairy

Hemyock on 25 May 1929. 1300's train includes two of the ex-Manchester & Milford carriages. It appears to have been the practice at this time to marshall goods wagons between two carriages. Only that next to the engine would have had the benefit of vacuum braking, so presumably carried the passengers whilst the other acted as brake van.

H. C. CASSERLEY

CULM VALLEY BRANCH.

Single Line worked by Train Staff and only one Engine in Steam at a time.   The Train Staff Stations are Tiverton Junction and Hemyock.

Distance		DOWN TRAINS.	Station No.	Week Days only.										UP TRAINS.	Week Days only.										
				1 B Mixed.		2 B Mixed		3	4 B Mixed.		5 B Passenger.				1 B Mixed.		2 B Passenger.		3 B Mixed.		4	5 B Passenger.		
M.	C.			arr.	dep.	arr.	dep.		arr.	dep.	arr.	dep.			arr.	dep.	arr.	dep.	arr.	dep.		arr.	dep.		
				A.M.	A.M.	P.M.	P.M.		P.M.	P.M.	P.M.	P.M.			A.M.	A.M.	A.M.	A.M.	P.M.	P.M.		P.M.	P.M.		
		Tiverton Junction	1538	—	9 0	..	12 10	..	—	4 0	—	6 25		Hemyock	—	7 25	—	11 0	—	2 50	..	—	5 25		
2	14	Cold Harbour Siding	1610											Whitehall Siding											
2	62	Uffculme	1611	9 12	9 27	12 22	12 32	....	4 12	4 27	—	6 38		Culmstock ..	7 55	8 1	11 11	—	3 0	3 6	...	—	5 36		
4	79	Culmstock ..	1612	9 36	9 50	12 41	12 50	..	4 36	4 50	—	6 48		Uffculme	8 10	8 18	11 20	11 23	3 15	3 23	...	5 45	5 47		
6	34	Whitehall Siding	1613	C R										Cold Harbour Sdg	C R										
7	27	Hemyock ..	1615	10 5	—	1 5	....	5 5	—	6 58				Tiverton Junct.	8 30	—	11 35	—	3 35	—		6 0	—		

Extract from the Regulations made by the Board of Trade for the working of the Culm Valley Light Railway:—
"This railway shall be worked between Tiverton Junction and Hemyock Station by means of one Engine in steam carrying the staff; that the rate of speed of the Trains shall not exceed fifteen miles an hour on any part of the said Railway; and that the Locomotive Engines, Carriages and Vehicles used on the Railway shall not have a greater weight than eight tons upon the rails on any one pair of wheels."
Long Round Timber.—Long Round Timber must not be accepted for transit at Uffculme, Culmstock or Hemyock.

GWR Working timetable, issued October 1920.

Company was feeling the pressure of low priced Commonwealth imports. At the same time changes in the London milk market saw the emergence of a powerful new force in the dairy industry. In 1915 Wilts United Dairies merged with the Great Western and Metropolitan Dairies to form United Dairies. The new company had half the wholesale trade in London and set about an aggressive policy of aquiring other dairy enterprises. Devon was so far from London as to make the transport of fresh milk to the capital only marginally worthwhile, so any base for milk collection needed to have an alternative means of utilising the milk when there was a surplus. The Culm Valley Dairy was ideal and an offer was made to purchase the company, along with a threat to open a rival dairy. The four founders of the CVDC were still the joint managing directors and accepted £9,000.

United Dairies stopped making butter and concentrated on milk collection for human consumption although some cheese was manufactured from time to time. The milk was sent out by rail, of course, in 17 gallon churns to rail linked depots on the west of London. The large churns were, in fact, preferred by railwaymen over the smaller 10 gallon churns then being introduced for road transport. The larger churn was easier to handle and an experienced man could roll two empty ones at once. The smaller churn was easier to lift onto a lorry, however.

In 1920 a new factory block was built for the manufacture of condensed milk, which became increasingly important, and agreement was made for a further link to be made into the factory by extending the main running line

from the station across the road. From 1922 to 1928 it was leased to Milkal Ltd, a subsidiary of J. Lyons & Co., to produce dried milk. A major fire in 1923 destroyed much of the factory but it was rebuilt. Milk was handled in increasing amounts; 6,000 gallons daily in 1920 rose to 9,000 in 1930. Liquid milk had been despatched by passenger train but the dried milk went by goods, causing a drop in receipts for the branch.

England after the Great War was a changed place and the transport field was one area where the change was particularly apparent. The war itself had prompted great developments in the petrol engined lorry and after the war many surplus vehicles became available. The milk factory commenced using lorries for farm collections in 1920 and elsewhere there was greater use of road transport. When Tiverton Shopping Week was advertised in December 1922 not only were times of trains from the Culm Valley stations given but so also were those of Croscols' buses from Uffculme. *Kelly's Directory* for 1926 noted a daily 'motor omnibus' from Uffculme to Tiverton Junction.

The Culm Valley branch does not seem to have been too badly affected initially by these changes. The traffic figures for 1923 show a drop in passenger figures to a little under 15,000; the losses occurring at Uffculme and Culmstock. Hemyock saw little change in its passenger figures over 20 years; perhaps being remoter the railway had less competition. Although the trains were a little faster – some took only 33 minutes to cover the line – the departure times for the branch had changed by only a few minutes from that of 1879 and one can but presume it was still meeting local needs. In 1920 the first down train, from Tiverton Junction, each day took no less than 65 minutes because it was allowed 12 to 15 minutes at the two intermediate stations for shunting freight. The mineral traffic had been lost but despite this the total goods carried were 20,000 tons, increases in all other types of traffic making up for the lack of stone business. Livestock traffic, too, increased well, particularly at Uffculme where in 1923 682 wagons were handled compared with 217 in 1913. The other two stations also showed increases.

Staff on the branch now numbered 13 with four, two and seven at Uffculme, Culmstock and Hemyock respectively. The new wages bill of £1,863 reflected another change that followed the war, whilst symptomatic of the different attitude of the working Briton was the need in June 1926 to introduce an emergency timetable of just three trains each way 'in consequence of Labour Troubles'. This was the general strike and all traffic ceased for a period until it was resolved.

During the summer of 1926 the goods shed was removed from the loop siding at Uffculme making possible, by the winter of that year, the introduction of an intermediate short working between Tiverton Junction and Uffculme. With a slight variation, this was to remain a feature

of the timetable until passenger services ceased. A couple of years later it was recorded that the branch handled 2,866 churns of milk and 1,185 trucks of livestock annually. On average one wagon of coal was dealt with each day, for domestic use as well as the mills, dairy and gas works, along with seven of general goods forwarded and eleven received. Inward traffic to the dairy included sealed vans from London Docks loaded with New Zealand butter to be blended with local produce. The principal outward traffic was meat and farm produce, including a surprising quantity of rabbits. The winter 1928 timetable included an early morning freight train leaving Hemyock at 5.30. This was allowed 36 minutes to get to Tiverton Junction, less than some passenger trains, although the return took 65 minutes after

Uffculme looking east, April 1926, clearly showing Pain's original goods shed with lamp room added as a lean-to. Inside was a 1 ton crane, the same as at Culmstock. In the left foreground is the middle ground frame. The wagons visible, cattle trucks, ventilated meat vans and George Small & Sons' coal truck, typify the traffic on the line at this time.

G. N. SOUTHERDEN,
COLLECTION M. J. MESSENGER

GWR 1300 at Hemyock, with the train crew and station staff, before 1920. In the frock coat, between the two porter-shunters with their shunting poles, is Mr Quick the station master. Behind him is the creamery chimney.

COLLECTION M. J. MESSENGER

CULM VALLEY BRANCH.

Single Line worked by Train Staff and only one Engine in Steam at a time.   The Train Staff Stations are Tiverton Junction and Hemyock.

DOWN TRAINS. Week Days only.

Dis-tance M.	C.	Station	Station No.	Ruling Gradient	K Goods arr.	dep.	B Mixed arr.	dep.	B Mixed arr.	dep.	B Mixed arr.	dep.	B Passenger R arr.	dep.	B Mixed Y arr.	dep.
		Tiverton Junction	1538			A.M. 6 20		A.M. 8 45		A.M. 11 40		P.M. 12 50		P.M. 4 30		P.M. 7 0
2	14	Cold Harbour Siding	1610	67 R.	R	R	8 56	9 12	11 51	—	1 1	1 7	4 41	4 46	7 11	7 16
2	62	Uffculme	1611	105 R.	6 51	6 51	9 21	9 35			1 16	1 22	4 54	4 56	7 25	7 26
4	79	Culmstock	1612	68 R.	7 0	7 10										
6	34	Whitehall Siding	1613	94 R.	C	R					C	R	C	R		
7	27	Hemyock	1615	76 R.	7 25	—	9 43				1 37		5 6		7 36	—

UP TRAINS. Week Days only.

Station	Ruling Gradient	K Goods arr.	dep.	B Passenger arr.	dep.	B Mixed Z arr.	dep.	B Mixed arr.	dep.	B Mixed arr.	dep.	B Passenger arr.	dep.
Hemyock	—		A.M. 5 30		A.M. 7 44		A.M. 10 25		P.M.		P.M. 2 45		P.M. 5 40
Whitehall Siding	76 F.	R	R										
Culmstock	94 F.			7 54	7 55	10 35	10 41			2 55	3 1	5 50	5 51
Uffculme	68 F.	C	R	8 4	8 5	10 50	10 58		12 10 V	3 10	3 18	6 0	6 5
Cold Harbour Siding	105 F.	C	R										
Stopboard 0M 23½ C	—		P		P		P		P		P		P
Tiverton Junction	67 F.	6 6		8 16	—	11 11		12 28		3 31	—	6 18	

Extract from the Regulations made by the Board of Trade for the working of the Culm Valley Light Railway:—

"This railway shall be worked between Tiverton Junction and Hemyock Station by means of one Engine in steam carrying the staff; that the rate of speed of the Trains shall not exceed fifteen miles an hour on any part of the said Railway; and that the Locomotive Engines, Carriages and Vehicles used on the Railway shall not have a greater weight than eight tons upon the rails on any one pair of wheels."

Long Round Timber.—Long Round Timber must not be accepted for transit at Uffculme, Culmstock or Hemyock.

R—To convey Meat Vans for Uffculme.   V—Not to convey wagons from Uffculme for Tiverton Junction.   Y—Wagons not to be detached or attached at Culmstock and not to convey more than 2 wagons for Hemyock.   Z—Not to exceed 10 wagons arriving Tiverton Junction.

GWR Working timetable, issued September 1928.

Fox's mill dominates the background behind Coldharbour Halt. The nameboard is as long as the simple wooden shelter and a quarter of the length of the sleeper built platform itself. 8 July 1957

R. M. CASSERLEY

shunting at Uffculme and Culmstock. This train ran only until the closure of Hemyock engine shed in October 1929.

The non-standard nature of the branch did catch GWR employees by surprise from time to time. During 1927 a horse box was sent to Hemyock by the afternoon train to collect a horse that was to go to Ireland, via Fishguard. The box was an old one and met the restriction of the reduced branch loading gauge. At Hemyock the oil lamp for the groom's compartment was lit and inserted in its hole in the roof. Alas, the extra nine inches height was sufficient to foul the overbridges near Tiverton Junction, smashing the lamp and dropping burning oil on to the hay and straw below. The train's arrival at the Junction, with the horse box belching flames and smoke, was dramatic but the horse was rescued and the fire put out before any damage was done.

The Great Western was very much aware of the changed trading conditions and commissioned a report on all its branch lines to examine their efficiency and to seek ways of making economies and improvements. The Hemyock branch came out quite well as there was a good surplus of receipts over costs. In 1925 the receipts were £22,609, although this was less than in 1924, and the costs were £7,857. Nevertheless the report concluded economies could be made and recommended transferring the passenger service to road and working the goods and milk traffic within an eight hour turn of duty. The engine shed and carriage shed were to go, as was the station master at Culmstock to give a total saving of £810 each year.

Surprisingly most of the report's recommendations were ignored; in fact the GWR set about a programme of improvements. The first came in January 1929 when it was agreed to provide a halt at Coldharbour at a cost of £111, and this was rapidly opened on 23 February 1929. In July the same year the GWR Traffic

Committee agreed to recommend to the Board that improvements should be made to the branch so that standard rolling stock could be used on it. Alterations were also planned at Culmstock and Hemyock stations and the total cost was £5,127. The directors approved the plans on 26 July 1927 and the following year the Engineering Committee recommended a further £1,100 for additional work.

October 1926 had seen 1298 withdrawn, in original condition, and relief was needed at times, particularly in 1928 when 1300 was away again at Swindon. Known visitors were 1192, 1196 and 1308. The first two were 2-4-0 side

tank locomotives built in 1866 by Sharp Stewart at Manchester for the Cambrian Railways. They were their Nos 57, once named *Maglona*, and 58, *Gladys*. 1192 was transferred from the Tanat Valley line to Exeter at the end of 1927 for the CVLR but was withdrawn in August 1929. Its sister engine, 1196, was also at Exeter for eighteen months from July 1927 and returned to Oswestry at the end of 1928.

Lady Margaret, 1308, had been acquired by the GWR in 1909 when they took over the working of the Liskeard & Looe Railway. *Lady Margaret* was also a 2-4-0 side tank and was built by Andrew Barclay, Sons & Co. Ltd. in

A Welsh train in Devon. Now GWR 1196, ex-Cambrian Railways No 58 GLADYS heads an ex-Manchester & Milford Railway carriage and train at Uffculme in 1927 or 1928. The structure to the right was a water tank for railway purposes.
COLLECTION AMYAS CRUMP

GWR 1308 LADY MARGARET on its brief visit to the branch in 1928. The carriage is unidentified.
Here, as in a number of photographs, can be seen how close the boundary fence is to the track and the lack of substantial ballasting or drainage. The light railway origins remained evident to the end.
B. Y. WILLIAMS, COLLECTION
M. J. MESSENGER

An un-identified GWR 0-4-2T of the 5800 class, possibly 5812, heads towards Uffculme about 1938. This is one of the few photographs to show one of the GWR clerestory coaches that worked on the line at this time.

B. K. Cooper, Millbrook House Collection

Culmstock, April 1926, before rebuilding. Although the main line has been relaid in bull-head track, a number of sidings are still in light flat bottom rail, spiked to the sleepers. The sign on the goods shed is an advertisement for Thorne Brothers' family drapery at Tiverton, whose signs appeared at most stations on the line.

G. N. Southerden, Collection M. J. Messenger

1902 at a cost of £1,570 for the LLR. She was rebuilt at Swindon in May 1929 and then had a short spell working on the Culm Valley line before transferring to Oswestry for the Tanat Valley.

Investigating the possibilities of electrification west of Taunton was one preoccupation of the GWR during the 1920s. One report, of June 1927, gave the option of using 'petrol cars' on the CVLR or of electrifying it, with sub-stations providing power at Culmstock and Hemyock.

The engine shed closed in October 1929, one aspect of the branch line report that was actioned, and the locomotive transferred to Tiverton Junction shed. However, the first passenger train of the day continued to start from Hemyock. To get the locomotive and carriages

there a freight train was scheduled to leave Tiverton Junction at about 6 a.m. and this continued to the end of the passenger service in 1963.

The 4800 (later 1400) class of standard GWR 0-4-2 side tanks was introduced in 1932 and soon found its way to the branch. A variant, 5812 of the similar 5800 class, was on the line for a few years from 1933. In May 1934 1300 was withdrawn and, once 5812 had left, until the end of steam the line was the exclusive preserve of the 4800 class. No other class of GWR locomotive was permitted on the line. The 4800 class was quite powerful for its size and was permitted to handle 140 tons up the grade to Hemyock and 180 tons back down. By comparison 1298 and 1300 had only been allowed to take 90 and 100 tons in each direction.

The improvements to the line that took place in the early 1930s were quite extensive. Like Uffculme, the layouts of the other stations were improved. A passing loop was installed at Culmstock. At Hemyock the carriage and engine sheds were removed and a much longer run round loop put in. These changes permitted newer GWR carriages to be used, although standard stock could still not be allowed, the branch being restricted to those vehicles specifically designated for it. The ex-M&MR carriages

Looking west from Uffculme showing what was latterly the only stop signal on the branch. The insulated meat vans on the left are on the private siding that served the slaughter house, later destroyed by fire and subsequently the site of Small's grain mill. Out of sight is the west ground frame. 6 April 1926.
G. N. SOUTHERDEN,
COLLECTION M. J. MESSENGER

were condemned; 3982 in 1930, 606 and 657 in 1936 and 1938 respectively. Some of the replacements were old clerestory stock.

The signalling in the mid thirties consisted almost entirely of distant signals protecting those level crossings approached by sharp curves from the west, since most stations were on the east side of the roads. Uffculme sported the only stop signal on the branch and also a distant for westbound trains. There is a record of a home signal at Culmstock in 1926. Lever frames were on the platforms, including at Tiverton Junction until that station was remodelled. The Junction did have home, starting and shunting signals for the branch, originally controlled from a box on the branch platform but latterly from the main line signal box.

Hemyock also had a ground frame in the extended yard.

A new telephone system replaced the old single needle telegraph in 1931 at a cost of £720 and a changed system of control was subsequently introduced. All stations and halts were instructed to telephone the next to advise of the departure of each train.

Whitehall halt was opened on 27 February 1933. The GWR at this time had a policy of providing facilities where-ever there was a prospect of additional passenger traffic and Whitehall and Coldharbour were two of many similar halts opened in the late-twenties and early-thirties. The decline in passenger numbers was arrested briefly and actually climbed a little in 1930, to 17,586. Uffculme was by far

Whitehall Halt and siding, looking west on 15 July 1958. The siding held but three wagons and locomotives were prohibited from it. The waiting shed is to the right of the crossing gate and the gatekeeper's tiny hut to the left.
R. M. CASSERLEY

GWR Public timetable for the summer of 1936.

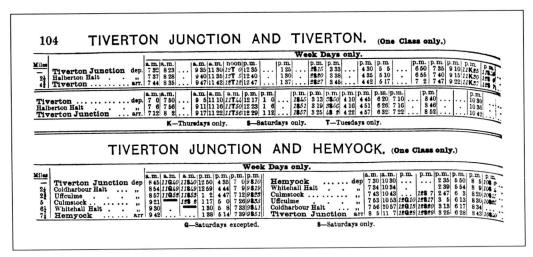

104   TIVERTON JUNCTION AND TIVERTON. (One Class only.)

Week Days only.

Miles		a.m.	a.m.		a.m.	a.m.	noon	p.m.		p.m.		p.m.	p.m.		p.m.	p.m.		p.m.	p.m.	p.m.	p.m.
—	Tiverton Junction .. dep.	7 32	8 23	...	9 35	11 30	12T 0	12 35	...	1 25	...	2S15	3 33	...	4 30	5 5	...	6 50	7 35	9 10	11K25
2¼	Halberton Halt .. .. "	7 37	8 28	...	9 40	11 35	12T 5	12 40	...	1 30	...	2S20	3 38	...	4 35	5 10	...	6 55	7 40	9 15	11K30
4½	Tiverton .. .. .. arr.	7 44	8 35	...	9 47	11 42	12T12	12 47	...	1 37	...	2S27	3 46	...	4 42	5 17	...	7 2	7 47	9 22	11K37

		a.m.	a.m.		a.m.	a.m.	a.m.	p.m.	p.m.		p.m.	p.m.	p.m.	p.m.	p.m.	p.m.	p.m.		p.m.		p.m.
	Tiverton .. .. .. dep.	7 0	7 50	...	9 5	11 10	11T44	12 17	1 0	...	1S45	3 13	3S50	4 10	4 45	6 20	7 10	...	8 40	...	10 30
	Halberton Halt .. .. "	7 6	7 56	...	9 11	11 16	11T50	12 23	1 6	...	1S51	3 19	3S56	4 16	4 51	6 26	7 16	...	8 46	...	10 36
	Tiverton Junction .. arr.	7 12	8 2	...	9 17	11 22	11T56	12 29	1 12	...	1S57	3 25	4S 2	4 22	4 57	6 32	7 22	...	8 52	...	10 42

K—Thursdays only.   S—Saturdays only.   T—Tuesdays only.

TIVERTON JUNCTION AND HEMYOCK. (One Class only.)

Week Days only.

Miles		a.m.	a.m.	a.m.	p.m.	p.m.	p.m.	p.m.				a.m.	a.m.	p.m.	p.m.	p.m.	p.m.	p.m.	p.m.
—	Tiverton Junction dep	8 45	11G40	11S40	12 50	4 35	7 0	8S10	Hemyock .. .. .. dep	7 30	10 30	...	...	2 35	5 50	8 10	
2¼	Coldharbour Halt .. "	8 54	11G49	11S49	12 59	4 44	7 9	8S19	Whitehall Halt .. .. "	7 34	10 34	...	...	2 39	5 54	8 14	
2¾	Uffculme .. .. "	8 57	11G53	11S53	1 2	4 47	7 12	8S23	Culmstock .. .. .. "	7 43	10 43	...	12S 7	2 47	6 3	8 20	10S
5	Culmstock .. .. .. "	9 21		12S 2	1 17	5 0	7 26	8S33	Uffculme .. .. .. "	7 53	10 53	12G10	12S17	3 5	6 13	8 30	10S
6½	Whitehall Halt .. "	9 30			1 30	5 8	7 33	8S41	Coldharbour Halt .. "	7 56	10 57	12G13	12S20	3 13	6 17	8 34	
7½	Hemyock .. .. .. arr	9 42	...		1 38	5 14	7 39	8S51	Tiverton Junction arr	8 5	11 7	12G23	12S30	3 25	6 28	8 43	10S

G—Saturdays excepted.   S—Saturdays only.

A loaded milk tank is free wheeled from the factory (to the right) into the station yard. Note the dairy employee riding on the vehicle. The occasion is a Culmstock Primary School visit in 1967.

W. H. HARRIS

the busiest station for passengers and no doubt Coldharbour halt helped the figures. Nevertheless the figures continued to decline and if one divides the passenger numbers by the number of trains running, on six days a week, an average of no more than a dozen passengers per train is arrived at.

The passenger service was at its peak in the 1930s with five trains from Tiverton Junction and six return workings; the morning freight being the balancing run. On Saturday nights a late train left the Junction soon after 9 p.m. and, in 1936 at least, returned from Hemyock as a timetabled passenger train at 10 p.m.

Freight traffic fared better, aided no doubt by the milk factory which must have accounted for much of the coal brought to Hemyock. Total tonnage handled was around 20,000 tons per year for much of the early part of the 1930s, despite the intense trade depression the whole country was experiencing. Livestock handled dropped substantially to only 351 wagons in 1934 and a contributory factor to this may have been the destruction by fire of the slaughter house at Uffculme but it also probably reflected the greater use of road transport for perishable goods. At this time Lloyd Maunder, at Tiverton Junction, were considering purchasing a fleet of lorries and cancelling their contracts with the GWR. To encourage traffic a confidential arrangement was made in

TIVERTON JUNCTION AND HEMYOCK.   (Week Days only.) (Third class only.)

			G	S									G	S				
		a.m.	a.m.	a.m.	p.m.	p.m.	p.m.	...			a.m.	a.m.	p.m.	p.m.	p.m.	p.m.	p.m.
Tiverton Junction ... dep.		8 45	11 35	11 35	1 30	4 32	7 10	...	Hemyock .. .. .. dep.	7 30	10 30	...	...	3 0	5 55	8 8	...
Coldharbour Halt .. .. "		8 54	11 44	11 44	1 38	4 41	7 19	...	Whitehall Halt .. .. "	7 34	10 34	...	...	3 5	6 0	8 12	...
Uffculme .. .. .. "		8 57	11 47	11 47	1 42	4 44	7 25	...	Culmstock .. .. .. "	7 41	10 43	...	12 10	3 13	6 8	8 20	...
Culmstock .. .. .. "		9 21		12 5	1 54	4 54	7 36	...	Uffculme .. .. .. "	7 50	10 53	12 10	12 19	3 25	6 18	8 30	...
Whitehall Halt .. .. .. "		9 30			2 3	5 2	7 44	...	Coldharbour Halt .. .. "	7 54	10 57	12 13	12 23	3 30	6 22	8 33	...
Hemyock .. .. .. arr.		9 42			2 10	5 8	7 50	...	Tiverton Junction arr.	8 2	11 7	12 23	12 33	3 40	6 33	8 42	...

Public timetable for the summer of 1947.

1932 with Small & Sons at Uffculme and with Hine at Hemyock to allow them 9d. a ton off the published rate so long as all their traffic was sent by rail. One of the important traffics to the branch was grain and oil cake from Avonmouth. During the thirties, at least, this amounted to nearly three-quarters of all the general traffic received at all three stations. In 1935 George Small built their grain mill on the former slaughter house site, west of Uffculme station, and this was to provide grain traffic for many years.

Liquid milk, from 1932, was carried in six-wheeled glass-lined 3,000 gallon tank wagons. The first of these had been introduced in 1927 as a joint venture between the GWR and United Dairies, the former providing the chassis and UD paying for the tanks. The necessity to get these to Hemyock may well have been another reason to upgrade the branch.

After rebuilding, the axle-loading limit on the branch was raised to 13 tons 18 cwts although the speed limit remained at 15 m.p.h. The loaded 20-ton grain wagons were exceptionally permitted as far as Small's private siding at Uffculme and the six-wheel milk tanks too had a specific exemption as all other six-wheel stock was banned. So were all vehicles over 60 feet in length and all ordinary passenger stock as the eight-wheeled carriages now in use were specially provided for the branch.

Only ten staff remained in 1934; two at Culmstock and four at each of the other stations. The wages bill was now £1,228 for the year.

As the country left the depression of the thirties behind, goods traffic climbed to a peak of 26,345 tons in 1938. The Second World War did little good to the branch line, despite military activity in the area, and from 1939 goods traffic steadily declined until by 1948 it was at little more than the level of 1879. Half of all traffic at this time was coal, for domestic use

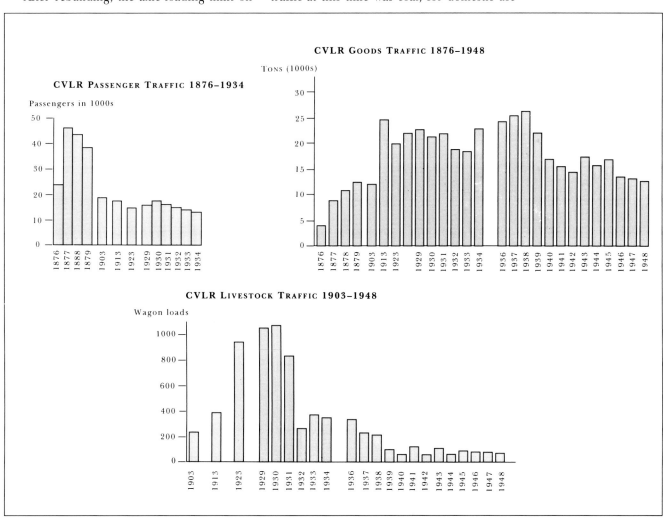

CVLR GOODS TRAFFIC 1876–1948

CVLR PASSENGER TRAFFIC 1876–1934

CVLR LIVESTOCK TRAFFIC 1903–1948

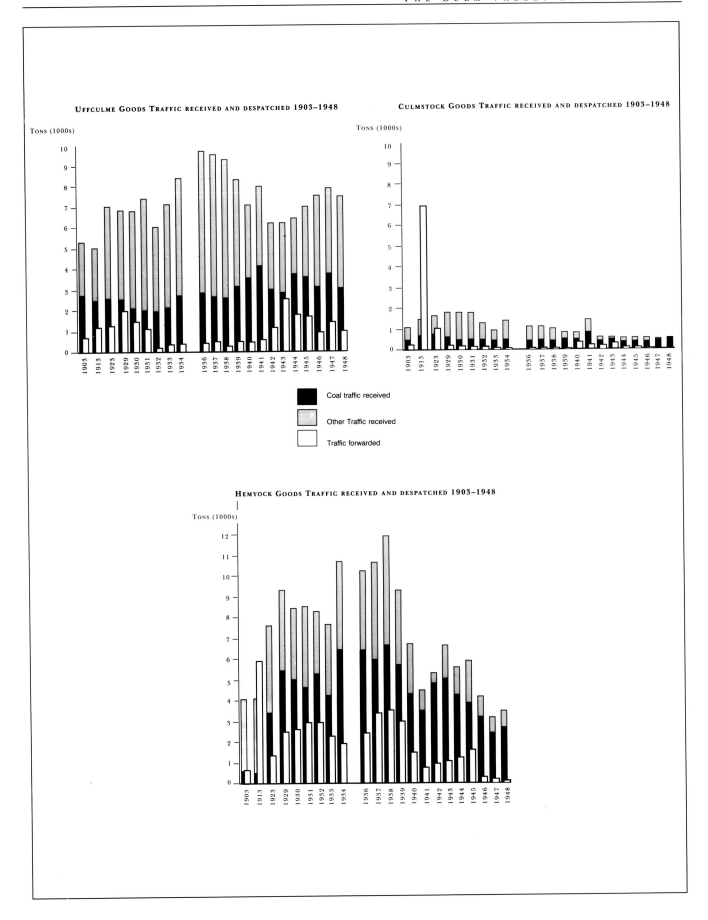

and for industry's use at the milk factory and Coldharbour mill. The milk factory, handling 12,000 gallons a day in 1940, diversified for the war effort into dried eggs and milk powder. Livestock almost fizzled out and the branch saw only one or two cattle trucks a week from 1939 onwards. Figures for passengers are not available but there can be little doubt that these too dwindled away.

Nationalisation brought little change for the branch. It has been said that for a brief period the line was allotted to the Southern Region of British Railways due to its geographical position south of the former GWR main line but such nonsense was soon remedied.

Reverting to the tradition of using carriages from the minor Welsh railways taken over by the GWR, early in 1950 the elderly GWR carriages were replaced by two ex-Barry Railway coaches. These had been built in 1920 and were now specially rebuilt at Swindon with gas lighting. The slow speeds on the branch were insufficient for the axle driven generators usually used to keep carriage batteries charged up, so these two carriages were to be the last gas lit vehicles on British Railways. They were 54 feet 6 inches long, 8 feet 9 inches wide and weighed

26 tons. They also acted as brake vehicles for the milk traffic and were it not for the need to include a carriage at the end of each train the passenger service would have ceased. As has been speculated elsewhere, one wonders why a battery charger could not have been installed, particularly as few trains ran after dark.

About 1955 much of the track was relaid. The milk factory was now using oil for fuel and this came by rail from Avonmouth. A report of this time notes an average of five passengers a day from Hemyock although more were carried from Uffculme, in the form of school children going to Tiverton. One suspects a good proportion of the passengers were railway enthusiasts for the branch was already well known as a novelty and a rare survival.

Although perhaps taken for granted and under used the line was very much a day-to-day feature of valley life and an important part of the local scene. An example that demonstrates this was the coded whistles used by the train drivers, before the local schools had telephones, to warn the headmasters that the train was carrying a visiting schools inspector from Exeter.

Economies were made in 1960 when Culmstock was unstaffed and reduced to the

Ex-Barry Railway coach converted to gas lighting and transferred to the Culm Valley. Built in 1920, it was 54 feet 6 inches long and carried British Railways, Western Region number W268W. Its sister was W263W. 11 August 1962.
M. J. MESSENGER

51

status of a halt. About the same time the gate-keepers were withdrawn and, except at Uffculme where the staff continued to perform the duties, the train crews operated level crossing gates. A Sunday service had been run since at least 1948 for milk traffic only, and now left Tiverton Junction at 2.00 p.m. and returning at 3.30 p.m. In 1948 there had been a morning train also, leaving the Junction at 8.15 a.m. although the engine came back light and returned light in the afternoon to bring the loaded milk tanks back.

It was not surprising when, early in 1962, closure notices were posted announcing the withdrawal of passenger services. Only Uffculme and Hemyock were to remain open for parcels and freight traffic. By then only these two stations were staffed and the Uffculme station master also controlled Hemyock. Passenger receipts were less than £1,000 and the £2,489 working expenses of providing the passenger service would be saved. It was also claimed that the coaches were obsolete and could not be replaced with modern vehicles, the gas lighting aspect being mentioned as if to emphasise their antiquity.

Despite this claim in the same year the ex-Barry coaches were replaced by two ex-London & North Eastern Railway carriages, due to the difficulty in maintaining gas supplies. The lighting problem was solved by running the carriages down to Exeter once a fortnight to charge up the batteries. These carriages were to work the final trains on Saturday 7 September 1963. Both were used and to accommodate the extra passengers benches from Tiverton Junction's waiting room were put in one of the guards vans. Some one hundred people were on the last train, although most appear to have been enthusiasts from away rather than local people. The last train, with the inevitable couple of milk tanks, left Hemyock a few minutes later than the advertised 6 p.m., hauled by 1421 and driven by J. Fewings, who had worked on the line for 18 years, and fired by E. Laskey.

It was not thought necessary to provide any replacement bus service. The Culm Valley passenger trains had been little noticed when they ran and they were, alas, no more missed as a public service in their absence. As a railway equivalent of the bucolic rural character, however, their passing was to be regretted. The line had become the epitome of a rural idyll, an English country branch line, and such rare breeds were rapidly to become extinct.

Awaiting the last train at Hemyock on 7 September 1963. Dare one say the station had not seen such a crowd since 1876? The enthusiasts are readily apparent but for how many local families was this their first and last visit to the station?

C. L. CADDY

CHAPTER FIVE

DECLINE AND CLOSURE

'Obviously charm alone cannot justify the retention of an unremunerative branch line'.
R. C. RILEY, 1962.

The 1960s was a time of great change in the British railway network. For many people this was epitomised by the end of steam but the changes were much more extensive than a mere change in motive power. The end of passenger trains and of steam on the Culm Valley Light Railway very much marked the end of an era, for this was the end of a manner and style of working that had altered but little since the opening of the railway in 1876. For eighty seven years a small steam engine, with a carriage or two, always elderly and sub-standard, and a few wagons, had trundled slowly up and down the valley four or five times a day to a timetable that had varied surprisingly little. All

that changed overnight and whilst the essence of the railway lived on, it was in a different style.

Not only had the line ceased to carry passengers but only Uffculme and Hemyock remained open for goods. On Saturday 7 September 1963 D2140, a small 204hp diesel locomotive, of a type introduced by BR in 1957, waited at Tiverton Junction to take over what was to be a daily freight service on the following Monday. Without station staff the train crew were expected to open all the level crossing gates as they proceeded up the valley. The whole branch fell under the responsibility of the Tiverton Junction signalman. Occasionally

British Railways D2119 passes Uffculme on the return to Tiverton Junction, 29 April 1967. The west facing end wall of the station building, like that at Culmstock, had been rebuilt without the timber framing by the 1920s.

M. J. MESSENGER

A vintage scene at Uffculme. D2119 crosses Bridge Street taking full milk tanks back down the valley to Tiverton Junction. The author's Morris Minor, parked in front of Small's, the Duple bodied bus, the Standard Vanguard and even Regent Oil are now items of nostalgia but Bridge House, St Mary's church and Furze's brewery all still survive, little changed. 29 April 1967.
M. J. MESSENGER

A North British type 2 diesel hydraulic at Hemyock in the 1960s, a scene little changed since steam days.
CHRIS TILLEY

With extra brake vans added to the rear for the benefit of an RCTS party, 7676 takes a loaded milk train down the valley through Uffculme on 13 October 1973. By this date the station buildings have been demolished and weeds have taken over the platform.

R. A. LUMBER

steam returned; a 1400 class would substitute for a broken down diesel locomotive.

During October and November the sidings were removed from Coldharbour, Culmstock and Whitehall and as the modernisation of British Railways progressed so the facilities further whittled away. Two years later on 6 September 1965 Hemyock closed for all traffic, apart from that from the milk factory, and Uffculme followed suit on 8 May 1967. At the latter George Small's siding remained, so the branch survived just to service the two private sidings.

Despite the declining traffic the trackwork was strengthened in order to take heavier locomotives, no doubt to simplify operations, and Hemyock became accessible to diesel hydraulic locomotives of class 29, earlier known in GWR fashion as the D6300 class. They had been built by the North British Locomotive Co. from 1959 and, at 68 tons, were the heaviest locomotives yet to work over the branch. Later class 22 diesel electrics, with the occasional class 35, were seen on the line. *The Railway Observer* in September 1971 described the traffic, grain from Uffculme and milk from Hemyock, as considerable. The grain wagons for Uffculme were propelled from Tiverton Junction. By now all the station buildings were demolished.

In the middle of the following year the track was being relaid, with flat-bottomed rail,

an unwitting reversion to the original type of rail used but somewhat heavier. New level crossing gates were hung at Whitehall and new signs put up at all the level crossings. Despite this the end of the year saw the first rumours of closure, linked to the plans for the M5 motorway although provision was made for a bridge over the branch.

The branch dallied on until 1975 in spite of losing both the grain and milk traffic to road. The milk factory relied on the railway to bring its oil in from Avonmouth and this was now the sole purpose of the line. Trains ran as they were required. When it was announced that Unigate were closing the factory on 31 October 1975 that sealed the fate of the branch. Empty milk tanks had been kept at Hemyock in case of emergency and most of these were removed by diesel locomotive 25094 on 20 August, delayed for a couple of days because motorway construction work had covered the track at Tiverton Junction. The remaining seven milk tanks were removed by a class 08 diesel electric shunting locomotive on 31 October 1975, the last traffic over the railway, just seven months short of achieving its centenary.

A little over a year later, by January 1977, the track had all been lifted so the Culm Valley Light Railway can be said, in one way or another, to have lasted until its centenary.

A sad scene of decay as the weeds and undergrowth slowly take over the rusting track. Note the check rail on the sharp curve; many sections of the line had these, originally at the insistence of Colonel Yolland following his inspection.

Chris Tilley

Two train staffs from the Hemyock Branch, now in a private collection. The earlier one, above, was formerly used on the Newham Branch in Cornwall, and was coloured red. The lower staff, with key, was in use at least by 1911.

Amyas Crump

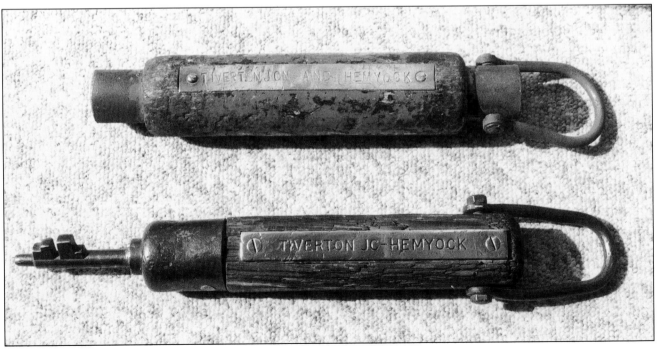

CHAPTER SIX

THE JOURNEY UP THE VALLEY

'The line itself has a quaint charm all of its own'.
THE RAILWAY OBSERVER, 1963.

Quite what arrangements were originally intended for the junction of the CVLR with the B&ER at Tiverton Junction are not known. The deposited plans merely show a line curving in from the east into the station forecourt. At this time the B&ER was broad gauge so a physical connection would not have been possible and some sort of interchange or transhipment for goods necessary.

As it was the B&ER had laid a third rail from Taunton to Exeter in 1876 and from March standard gauge trains could reach Exeter so from the outset the CVLR had a connection to the national network. The light railway ran into Tiverton Junction, crossing the Willand to Halberton road by widening the B&ER bridge, to use the east side of the down platform. No run round was provided but the line continued into the goods yard where, by

passing through the goods shed, it was possible for the engine to run round a train. It was more convenient to back the train down the branch, up the start of the climb out of the Junction, detach the engine into a short siding and run the train downhill past it by gravity. When the main line station was rebuilt in 1932, with quadruple tracks passing through the station, a direct connection from the branch to the main line platform road was put in. The short refuge siding was taken out, putting an end to gravity shunting. At this time traces of the widened bridge over the Halberton road disappeared. Tiverton Junction station closed with the opening of Tiverton Parkway, a short distance to the north, on 12 May 1986, although because of engineering work over the weekend the last train to actually call at the Junction was on Friday 9 May. The station buildings were

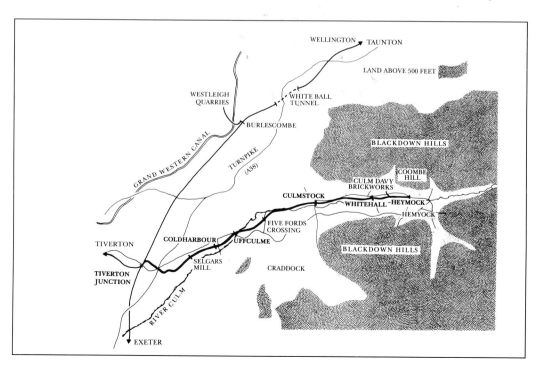

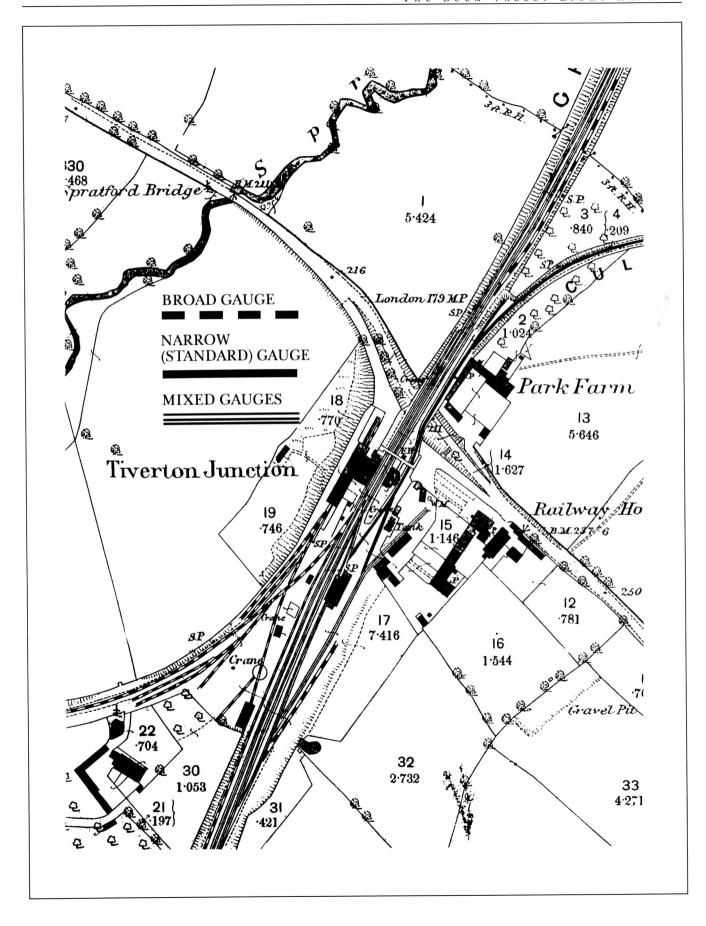

BROAD GAUGE

NARROW
(STANDARD) GAUGE

MIXED GAUGES

Tiverton Junction

Park Farm

Railway Ho

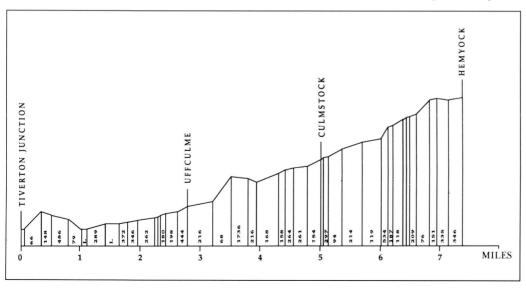

The Parliamentary Plan of 1873 showed the CVLR curving into Tiverton Junction alongside the then broad gauge B&ER and without a physical connection.

subsequently demolished, although in 1992 the platforms remained.

Leaving Tiverton Junction the branch train was facing almost north east but immediately entered a 10 chain radius curve that was to take the line through about 90 degrees until it was heading almost south east. At the same time the line was climbing at 1 in 66 and immediately

the traveller was left in no doubt as to the nature of this railway. $23\frac{1}{2}$ chains (517 yards) from the Junction a stop board instructed all up trains to stop. This was not only a precaution against the falling gradient but to protect any shunting that might be happening at Tiverton Junction on the beginnings of the branch. Nearby was a timber overbridge, later replaced

The railway which commences at the Tiverton Junction and terminates at Hemyock is seven miles in length and passes through a good agricultural district. On leaving the junction there is a slight incline, the train is soon brought into the only deep cutting to be found throughout its entire length. This being passed, the country is open and the route lies through a very pleasant part presenting many attractive views. On the left peeping out between the dark foliage of tall trees, we catch a glimpse of Bradfield House, the seat of Sir J. W. Walrond. Shortly after we are brought close to the River Culm, but passing over a wooden bridge it is for a time lost sight of. That we are approaching the first station on the line after leaving the junction is evidenced by the sight of the central residences which stand in their own beautiful grounds looking out over the line, amongst which is that of G. M. Marker Esq., R. H. Clark Esq. and Lt. Col. Grey. After passing Selgar's Mills and the factory of Messrs Fox the Uffculme station is reached, situated on the right of the town, from which a good view of the church is obtained, and also the noted brewery of Mr Furze. Here several passengers were added and after detaching some goods trucks the train left the station.

The line in this part curves considerably, in fact the entire route is as tortuous as it is possible to conceive of and necessitates slower travelling than most people are accustomed to on a railway. Again in the beautiful open valley of the Culm, the train proceeds onward through some capital scenery, and shortly after a new brick building on the left side of the line, designed for the Culmstock School Board, which opens the approach to this once busy manufacturing place. At this station the tickets are collected and we are soon on the way to the last station on the line. The Culmstock beacon is a prominent object on the left of the line standing out darkly against the distant horizon, and soon after passing this we get a view of the Wellington monument. The tops of some of the hills in this part present a weird and barren appearance, whilst further down their sides and in the valley itself there is an abundance of verdant and luxuriant vegetation.

The train at length arrives at the Hemyock terminus of the line and judging from mere appearances the question may well be asked what has a railway to do here? The station is some distance from the village and only a few houses show up, with just a sight of the church to give proof that this is really an inhabited place. Each of the stations has been erected near the bridges which carry the public road over the River Culm and forms a very pretty lookout from these spots. This section of the line near Hemyock station, affords easy travelling and the scenery throughout is exceedingly pleasant. Few if any places are so highly favoured with a special line of railway as those of the Culm Vale Light Railway and it remains to be seen whether the enterprise will meet with the support which it deserves for this newly opened up district.

Description of the line abbreviated from the *Tiverton Gazette*, 30 May 1876.

In this view of 1451 pulling out of Tiverton Junction the curve of the Hemyock branch, as it turns and climbs away from the main line, can be clearly seen. The connection between the branch and main line was put in in 1932 and removed in 1964. The carriage is one of the ex-LNER short wheelbase pair. 15 June 1962.

R. C. RILEY

1449 at Tiverton Junction, just arrived from Hemyock, 23 July 1958.

R. C. RILEY

with a concrete beam, carrying a footpath. Although the bridge remains the cutting on either side has been almost entirely filled in. Beneath the concrete beam can still be seen some of the brickwork that supported the earlier bridge.

The climb took the train into Crossways cutting, the major engineering feature on the line. This was, and still is, spanned by two brick over bridges, one carrying the turnpike – now the B3181 (formerly the A38) – and the other the road to Halberton. After reaching a summit a gentle fall began towards the flood plain of the River Culm and near Jaycroft Farm a 6 chain radius curve turned the route easterly through another 90 degrees towards Quicks

Pulling up towards Crossways Cutting from Tiverton Junction, with the main line in the background, 1421 with one of the ex-LNER coaches on 3 November 1962.

PETER W. GRAY

The steam crane has lowered the new concrete beam into position replacing Pain's timber footbridge across Crossways cutting. The new bridge awaits its railings. This view is facing Tiverton Junction – the main line can be seen beyond – and beside the crane is the stop board instructing 'All up trains must stop dead here'. Beneath the beam, to the right of the track, two workmen sit on the brick foundation of Pain's bridge.
COLLECTION AMYAS CRUMP

1421 runs past Selgar's Mill pond with the 12.9 p.m. from Culmstock. 3 November 1962.
PETER W. GRAY

Farm. The descent quickened to 1 in 74 and by milepost 1 the line was on the plain, a position it rarely left.

More curves of 6 chains radius followed and Selgar's Mill was passed by a 10 chain sweep to the north of the mill. This resulted in the blind spot from the crossing that miller Brown complained of. The line now was heading generally north east and retained this direction for most of the rest of the route. Close to milepost 2 the tailrace of Coldharbour Mill, which was to become the leat feeding Selgar's Mill, had to be diverted by the railway on construction. The leat was crossed by a rivetted iron skew bowstring girder bridge which still stands, now carrying nothing but the occasional cow.

Soon Coldharbour Mill appeared on the north side of the line and in front of it was its eponymous siding. Coldharbour has been variously spelt as one or two words, even appearing with both spellings on the same page of some GWR publications. A simple siding (2 miles 14 chains from Tiverton Junction), holding nine wagons, on the north side of the line was provided, along with a small gatekeeper's hut to protect the crossing of the minor road from Smithincott.

Coldharbour Halt with 1421 arriving. 3 November 1962.
PETER W. GRAY

Cold Harbour Halt, nameboard
C. L. CADDY

The halt, opened on 23 February 1929, was of simple but solid timber construction with a short platform carrying a wooden waiting hut, a nameboard – reading 'COLD HARBOUR HALT' – and a concrete lamp post supporting an oil lamp. The tarmacked platform was but three or four times the length of the nameboard. Access to the platform was by a wicket gate through the sturdy wooden fence that separated railway property from the road. The crossing keeper's hut was a typical GWR design and presumably replaced Pain's in 1929. The siding was removed in October or November 1963. The site has been rased and is a car park for the working woollen museum that now keeps the mill alive.

After crossing the public road, on the level

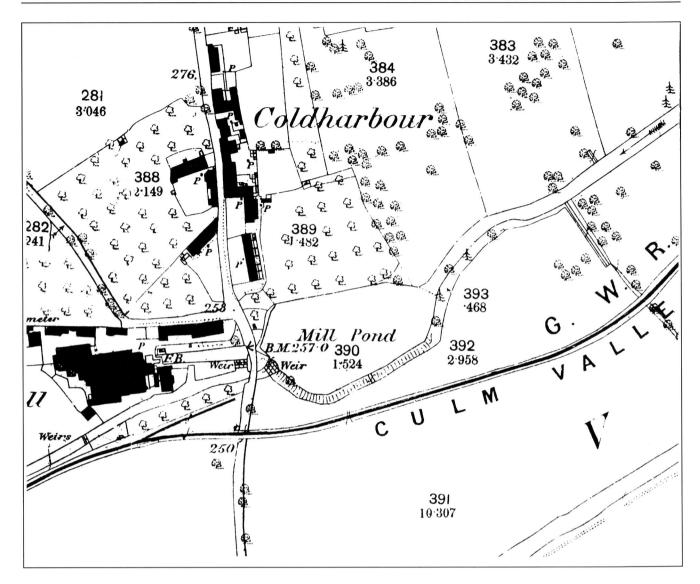

The approach for passengers to Coldharbour Halt, showing the wicket gate through the heavy timber fence. The crudely lettered departure time board suggests a local initiative.

LENS OF SUTTON

The gatekeeper opens the gates for road traffic as the 1.40 p.m. from Tiverton Junction leaves Coldharbour, 8 July 1959. The simple wooden construction of the timber platform can be clearly seen. The gatekeeper's hut is believed to date from 1929, when the halt was opened.

H. C. CASSERLEY

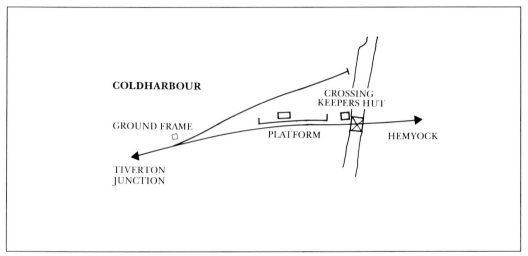

as were all remaining road crossings, the line passed close to the mill pond and leat and entered a series of reverse curves, many of 6 chains. It is often said that the CVLR had so many tight curves because it was built to skirt around the edges of fields. Whilst this may overstate the case the plans of the line do suggest that it was designed to avoid disrupting too many fields as the line was certainly built close to field boundaries or to the river.

Now a public footpath maintained by the Uffculme Trust, the stretch of trackbed onwards to that town passes over a small plate girder bridge. The approach to Uffculme is marked by the Lloyd Maunder animal feed mill, bought from George Small & Co. in 1976. It, like the slaughter house which previously

occupied the site, provided useful traffic for the railway and a private siding was provided by an agreement dated 9 October 1919. It was extended in 1949 at the same time as the mill building. Just beyond the points and the small ground frame for the siding was the only stop signal on the branch, protecting the road crossing of Bridge Street that gave Henry Bramley such concern. Passing immediately north of Uffculme Bridge the cramped site of Uffculme station was reached (2 miles 62 chains).

The station was particularly noted for its flower beds and the roses growing over the fencing and nameboard. The three station buildings were all of similar style, brick built with a distinctive timber framing and tiled roofs. Pain used the same design of building on

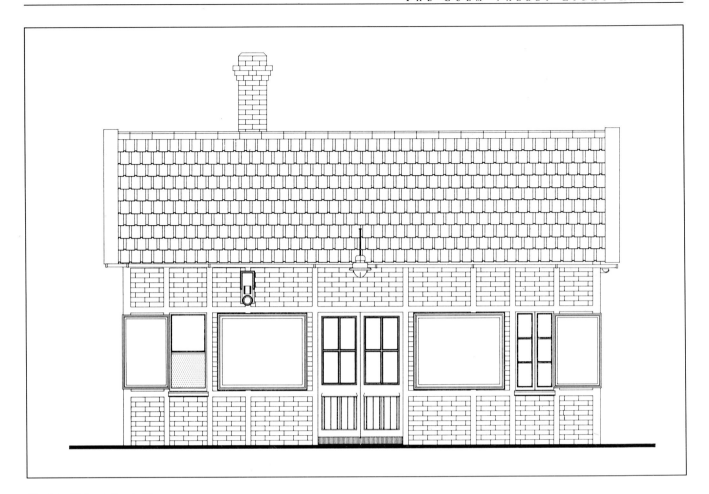

The Culm Valley station buildings that Pain designed were in a distinctive rural style, timber framed and with a pantiled roof. Although the drawing depicts Culmstock in its later days, with modified windows and poster boards covering the walls, Uffculme was almost identical. The same design was used almost without modification on the Southwold Railway and in a timber version on the Swindon & Highworth Light Railway. None survive, alas.

JOHN STENGELHOFEN

A busy scene at Uffculme, about 1930, with two of George Small's horse drawn carts in the goods yard and a third about to turn in. A lorry, presumably a GWR Thorneycroft, can be seen to the right of the cattle trucks. William Furze's brewery has not yet lost its chimney.

COLLECTION M. J. MESSENGER

STATION, UFFCULME.

both the Swindon & Highworth Light Railway and the Southwold Railway, although the former were timber clad. At Uffculme a loop siding passed through the small, 29 feet long, timber goods shed, making it unusable as a run round loop. A short siding off the west end of the loop served the cattle pens, conveniently

close to the road, and one of the other two sidings terminated in a carriage dock. The layout was altered a little in 1926 and was not touched again in the changes of the 1930s. The goods shed went and the loop became useful as a run round, enabling trains to terminate here. Empty coaching stock was permitted to be pro-

Uffculme with 1450 and short wheelbase ex-LNER coach W87245E in the last months of passenger services. The sister coach was W87270E; the W indicating Western Region allocation and the E LNER origin. On the left, across the road behind the cattle dock, is Small's grain mill, a useful source of traffic for many years.

M. J. FOX

1451 on the 2.45pm from Hemyock in Uffculme station 15 September 1962.

PETER W. GRAY

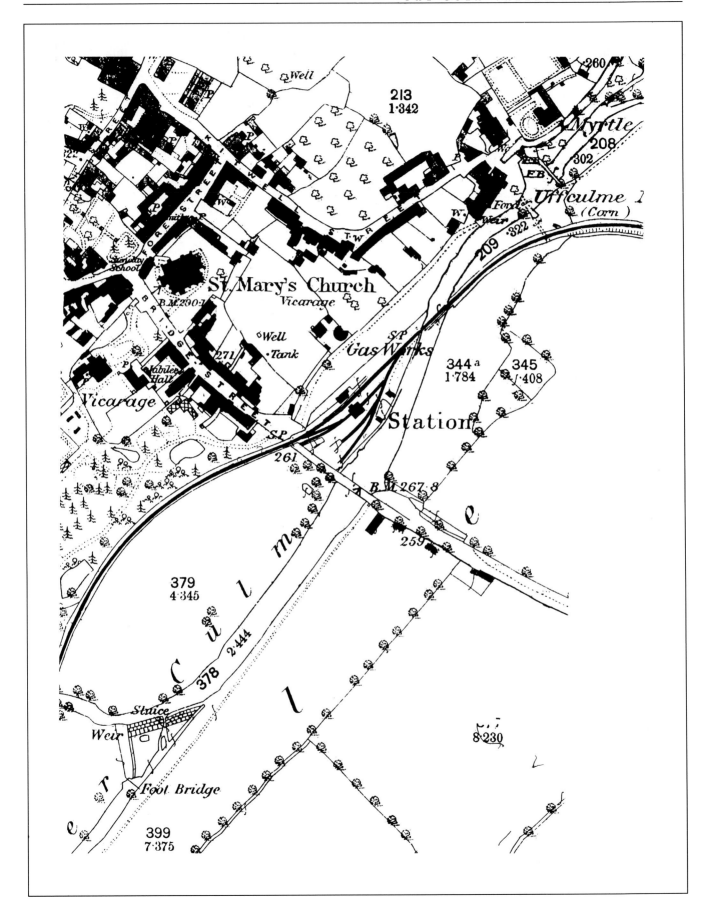

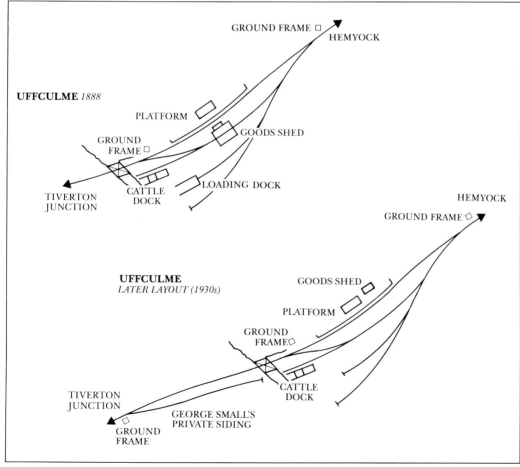

GROUND FRAME □
HEMYOCK

UFFCULME *1888*

PLATFORM

GROUND
FRAME □
GOODS SHED

TIVERTON
JUNCTION

CATTLE
DOCK
LOADING DOCK

HEMYOCK
GROUND FRAME □

UFFCULME
LATER LAYOUT (1930s)

GOODS SHED

PLATFORM

GROUND
FRAME □

TIVERTON
JUNCTION

CATTLE
DOCK

GEORGE SMALL'S
PRIVATE SIDING
GROUND
FRAME □

Uffculme from the air, taken in the mid-1960s. Small's mill is to the left, west, of the station but the gas works, behind the station, has been demolished. St Mary's is prominent in the centre and beyond is William Furze's brewery.

COLLECTION ALAN DIXON

Uffculme was noted for its colourful flower beds and the dahlias bloomed regardless of impending closure. 7 September 1963.

C. L. CADDY

Approaching Uffculme; 1451 in August 1962.

M. J. MESSENGER

pelled back to Tiverton Junction from here. A corrugated iron goods shed was installed on the platform by 1919. Only the cattle dock spur was removed at the end of 1963, the remaining sidings surviving until their removal about 1967. The platform kept its original length of 120 feet throughout its life.

Nothing now remains of Uffculme station, the site having been built upon. Immediately on leaving the station the River Culm was crossed for the first time. The six span timber

bridge was replaced in 1915 by a single span iron girder bridge. The route, now on the south side of the river, has been incorporated into fields on this stretch, since closure. Skirting Yondercott Farm the route climbed for about quarter of a mile at 1 in 68 to slightly higher ground. When the line opened Ratsash Lane was a public road and was crossed on the level at Five Fords Crossing. A crossing hut was provided here although it was not a block post. Here nowadays, one can visualise the line of the level crossing from remaining railway fencing and gateposts. The line then dropped gently until it was back alongside the river at Southey Barton.

The river is crossed, at 4 miles 28½ chains from Tiverton Junction, on a three span plate girder bridge, built on the skew, that still survives in apparent good order. Beneath the spans in the river bed can be found a few of the timber piles of Pain's original bridge. Now back on the north side of the river, a series of further reverse curves followed, and for a while the line stayed close to the river until, crossing the end of Culmstock Bridge, the station of the same name was reached. This section of the trackbed, from the bridge to the station, is now a footpath.

A train approaches Yondercott Farm, east of Uffculme, on a winter's day no later than the turn of the century. The original rails are now on square sleepers but the ballsting looks sparse.
HISTORICAL MODEL RAILWAY
SOCIETY

Culmstock gates are opened for the 1.45 p.m. from Tiverton Junction, hauled by 1451. 2 December 1961.
PETER W. GRAY

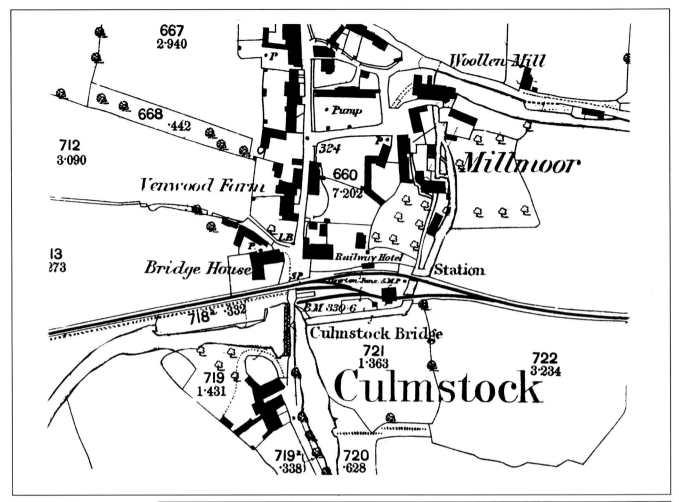

The three span girder bridge crossing the River Culm, five-eighths of a mile west of Culmstock, in the 1930s. The bridge still survives and beneath it can be found some remains of the timber pile bridge, built by Pain, that it replaced.

B. K. COOPER

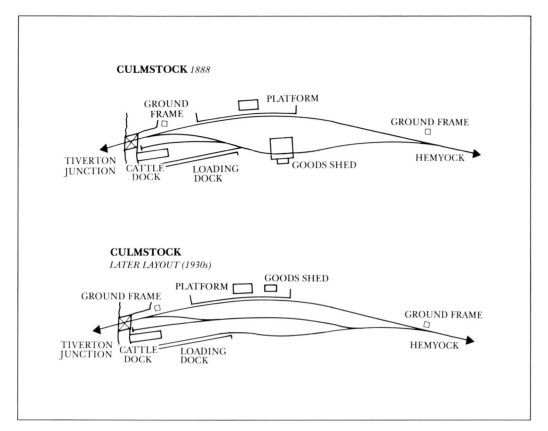

CULMSTOCK *1888*

GROUND FRAME
PLATFORM
GROUND FRAME
TIVERTON JUNCTION
CATTLE DOCK
LOADING DOCK
GOODS SHED
HEMYOCK

CULMSTOCK
LATER LAYOUT (1930s)

GROUND FRAME
PLATFORM
GOODS SHED
GROUND FRAME
TIVERTON JUNCTION
CATTLE DOCK
LOADING DOCK
HEMYOCK

The simple layout at Culmstock (4 miles 79 chains) consisted of a loop siding passing through the goods shed, as at Uffculme, and a couple of short sidings off the loop serving the cattle dock. The platform and goods shed were of the same sizes as Uffculme. The layout changed quite drastically when rebuilt, with a new loop running parallel to the main line. Part of the old loop remained as a siding. The goods shed went in favour of a standard GWR corrugated iron building on the platform, although it differed from Uffculme in having a peaked roof instead of a curved one. These alterations took place by the summer of 1930, permitting the short working to Uffculme to continue to Culmstock on Saturdays. All sidings

1466 pulls into Culmstock with an ex-Barry Railway coach.
M. J. FOX

The morning short working has arrived at Culmstock and 1421 runs round ready to become the 12.9 p.m. back to Tiverton Junction. 3 November 1962.
PETER W. GRAY

were removed at the end of 1963 and the site is now part of the Culm Valley Inn car park; formerly the Railway Hotel. Part of the loading bank wall forms the southern boundary of the car park. Above the station is Culmstock Mill, now converted into dwellings, which was built as a woollen mill by Fox Bros. in the 1870s and later occupied by the Culm Valley Dairy Co. The mill tailrace here was diverted in the construction of the station. There was a steady climb alongside the mill leat, away from the river at first and then close to. Half a mile east a 40 feet span girder bridge replaced a timber bridge over a stream in 1922. Another minor public road was crossed and Whitehall was reached.

The short siding here (6 miles 34 chains) only held three wagons and was put in when

Culmstock nameboard was in blue emamel. 7 September 1963.
C. L. CADDY

the CVLR was opened. Despite many attempts by Edward Lutley to have a passenger platform, nothing happened until the GWR opened Whitehall Halt on 27 February 1933. The timber faced platform was even shorter than at Coldharbour with just a nameboard. The small wooden hut was at ground level between the wicket gate and the platform. An even smaller

1451 eases its train across the level crossing at Culmstock, 25 May 1952.
R. J. SELLICK COLLECTION, NATIONAL RAILWAY MUSEUM

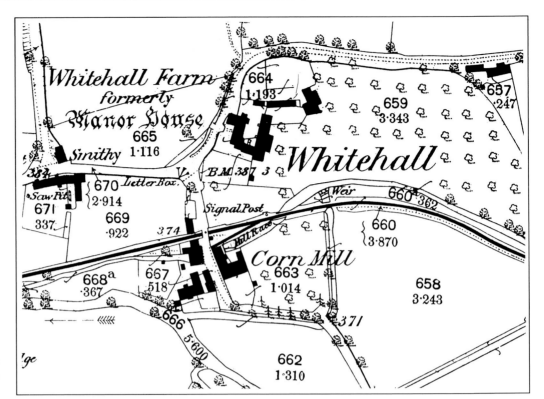

The fireman opens the gates at Whitehall on 4 November 1961 for the 3 p.m. from Hemyock. Even after closure to passengers, here and at Coldharbour, newspapers were left in the waiting shed for collection by local residents.

PETER W. GRAY

wooden hut on the opposite side of the track was provided for the gatekeeper. Locomotives were prohibited from working into the siding which was taken out of use on 28 October 1963 and removed the following month. The short platform remains, grassed over, and a notice on the field gate gives a brief history. Alongside survives the wicket gate that used to take passengers to the station.

Yet more reverse curves at the tight 6 chains radius took the line now in an easterly direction. The end of the siding into Culm Davy brickworks was passed with only an odd alignment of the fencing and faint traces in the field beyond to show where it had been. All that can be detected where it crossed the road from

Whitehall Halt nameboard, 7 September 1963.

C. L. CADDY

Whitehall to Millhayes, are the bridge abutments in the stream alongside. There is no visible trace in the field north of the road but the few buildings, now in agricultural use, do betray their origin as a brick works. Back alongside the river again, the terminus of the CVLR was reached at Millhayes.

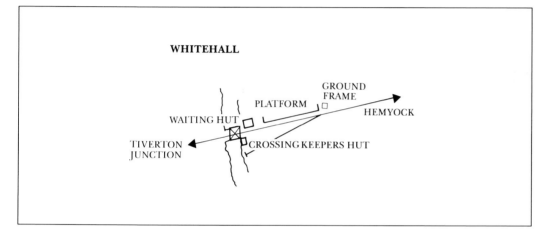

The passenger's approach to Whitehall; the wicket gate, far left, leading eastwards past the shelter onto the gravel surfaced timber platform. The timetable board is neater than Coldharbour's but blank!

LENS OF SUTTON

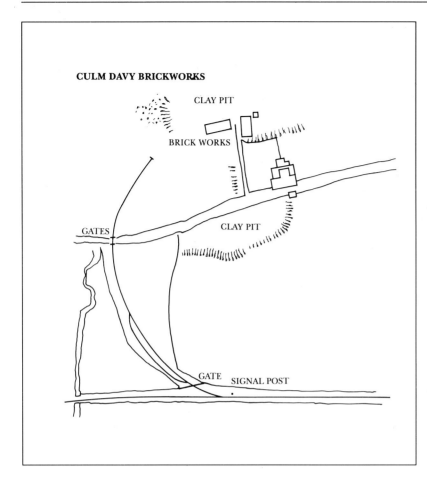

CULM DAVY BRICKWORKS

CLAY PIT

BRICK WORKS

CLAY PIT

GATES

GATE   SIGNAL POST

Hemyock station (7 miles 27 chains) is about 400 feet above sea level, some 140 feet above Tiverton Junction, and saw more changes than the other stations. The cramped site alongside the river may have been all the company could afford but it probably sufficed in the early days. The short platform and station building was beyond an extremely short run round loop. The engine shed trailed back from the loop and a siding ran off the loop to the timber goods shed. Trailing back from this siding another ran to the carriage shed, also built of timber. At the engine shed was an open coaling stage and a column water tank. The station building, like the others, was of red brick with timber framing and a red tile roof. It was slightly larger than the other stations and contained the usual booking and parcels offices and lavatories. A small signal box was at the west end of the building. Behind the station building, beyond railway property, was the stone building that was briefly the refreshment room.

Within a few years of opening a cattle dock was provided and the goods shed line was extended across the road to Millhayes Mill. By 1904 the mill siding branched within the mill

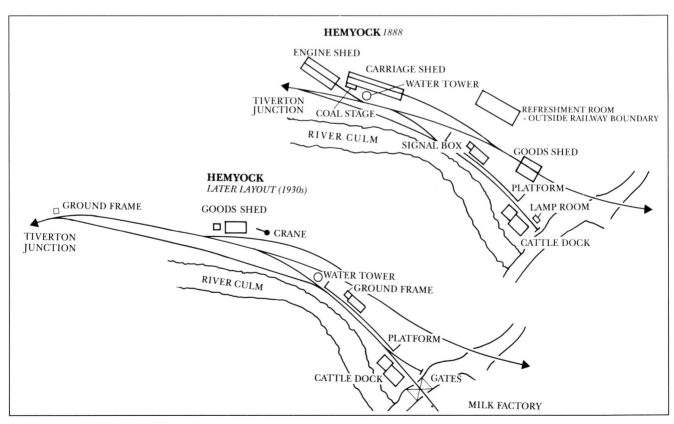

HEMYOCK 1888

ENGINE SHED

CARRIAGE SHED

WATER TOWER

TIVERTON JUNCTION

COAL STAGE

REFRESHMENT ROOM - OUTSIDE RAILWAY BOUNDARY

RIVER CULM

SIGNAL BOX

GOODS SHED

PLATFORM

LAMP ROOM

CATTLE DOCK

HEMYOCK
LATER LAYOUT (1930s)

GROUND FRAME

GOODS SHED

TIVERTON JUNCTION

CRANE

RIVER CULM

WATER TOWER

GROUND FRAME

PLATFORM

CATTLE DOCK

GATES

MILK FACTORY

A fine view across the station and yard at Hemyock. October 1951.

R. J. SELLICK COLLECTION, NATIONAL RAILWAY MUSEUM

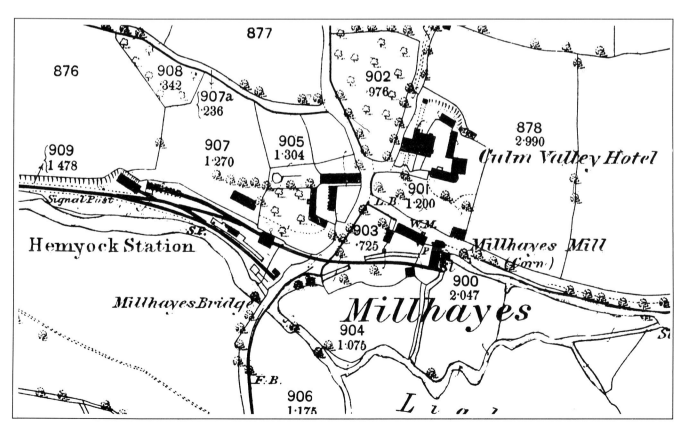

An almost deserted Hemyock station in July 1948. On the left the goods shed and yard crane installed in the 1930s, replacing the original 30 feet long goods shed with its 30 cwt crane. The water tank was moved from beside the engine shed to the position seen.

R. J. SELLICK COLLECTION,
NATIONAL RAILWAY MUSEUM

Hemyock station building on 11 August 1962. Comparison with the photograph on page 29 reveals the alterations made over time to the building, with doors replacing windows and vice versa. The change from brickwork to concrete block in the platform face marks where it was realigned in 1920. The block built extension at the east end dates from the same time. The signal cabin carried the legend Hemyock East Ground Frame from the 1930s.

M. J. MESSENGER

grounds to a second siding, the mill tailrace being diverted to make way for it. In 1920 an additional siding was put in to what had by then become the milk factory at Millhayes. This was done by extending the platform road past the cattle dock. The platform end was realigned to one side to permit a short dead end spur to be provided, and this probably shortened the platform slightly to 118 feet. Opposite the cattle dock was a small timber framed, brick building of obvious Pain design and similar to the crossing keeper's hut he provided the Swindon & Highworth Light Railway. It lasted at least until the 1920s.

The midday mixed train has just arrived at Hemyock behind 1300. April 1926.
G. N. SOUTHERDEN,
COLLECTION A. A. JACKSON

Looking east from the platform at Hemyock in April 1926. The small building, a lamp room, opposite the cattle dock is timber framed and of a similar style to one on the Swindon & Highworth Light Railway. It was subsequently demolished.
G. N. SOUTHERDEN,
COLLECTION M. J. MESSENGER

Hemyock nameboard, 7 September 1963.

C. L. CADDY

The major change, however, came shortly after 1930 when the whole of the station layout west of the station was revised. The engine shed had been closed on 21 October 1929 and both it and the carriage shed went. In their place a more sensibly sized run round loop was installed. On the north side of the running line a further loop siding served a new corrugated iron goods shed. At the same time a ground frame was put in at the western extremity of the station layout, named Hemyock West Ground Frame, and the nameboard on the signal box on the platform changed to Hemyock East Ground Frame. The signals had disappeared soon after the turn of the century so the box's title of signal box had become something of an anachronism.

The original level crossing, to the north,

was not protected by gates and locomotives were not permitted to cross the road. Shunting could be done by attaching additional wagons between the engine and those needing to go to and be drawn from the factory. The engine was permitted to cross the road at the other (southerly) crossing, which did have gates. Keys to the gate were held by milk factory staff who were also responsible for protecting both crossings. Neither could be used except in daylight. In practice the milk tank wagons were winched across by the diary staff and returned to the station by gravity. Wheel stops were fixed on the station side of both crossings and the keys held at the station.

The layout remained as the 1930s left it until the total closure of the branch in 1975. The site has now been cleared completely and is used as a car park for the factory. Part of the wall of the loading bank and the former builders merchant's store are all that survive although across the road, by the factory building, is a short length of track set into concrete. Nearby the later goods shed is in farm use.

Some six months after closure a new use was found by the factory's owners and the 'milk factory' now produces the nation's supplies of St Ivel Gold, a butter substitute. All distribution is by road, however.

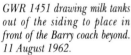

GWR 1451 drawing milk tanks out of the siding to place in front of the Barry coach beyond. 11 August 1962.

M. J. MESSENGER

CHAPTER SEVEN

CONCLUSIONS

As a pioneer light railway the Culm Valley Light Railway cannot be said to have been an outstanding success although, to be fair, there was an unintentional conspiracy against it.

Whilst the B&ER were very supportive they insisted upon proper stations with buildings and platforms and could not reduce their ideas of the motive power and rolling stock to Pain's concept. The attitude of the Board of Trade that a railway must meet certain standards did not help either. This is exemplified by the objection to the platforms not being long enough for six coach trains when it must have been readily apparent that the district would not generate such traffic, even for small four wheel carriages. Although the legislation was there, there was no apparent willingness by the railway 'establishment' to encourage light railways.

The Great Western certainly had no inclination to operate the line as a light railway and wanted standardisation in order for it to fit in with their existing system. This is understandable bearing in mind that they were not involved in the original plans to build the line as a light railway and had operational considerations to the fore.

Had Pain elected to build the line to a narrower gauge, such as three feet as he subsequently adopted for the Southwold Railway, there might have been a readiness to accept lower standards. Ground level platforms and

This view of Blythburgh station on the Southwold Railway, in Suffolk, taken about 1900, shows clearly the similarity in station design. This three feet gauge railway, completed a few years after the Culm Valley Light, demonstrates the evolution of Arthur Pain's thinking on light railways. The simplicity of the station arrangements and the goods shed and platform, left, represents an extension of his original ideas for the Culm Valley.

SOUTHWOLD MUSEUM

simple shelters were more acceptable as, from some viewpoints, narrow gauge lines were not 'proper' railways. Locomotives and rolling stock could have been more suited to the line's actual needs. The initial cost might well have been lower too, although the company may have had to purchase its own locomotives and rolling stock, and the independent company could have survived somewhat longer. Transhipment would have been a small handicap and the volumes of traffic could have endured the break of gauge at least until the milk tanks were introduced in the 1930s. By then continental style transporter wagons were well enough known and could have met that need, as they did on the 2 feet 6 inches gauge Leek & Manifold Valley Light Railway, in Derbyshire, from 1904. One deduces from Pain's later writings that he, too, came to believe a narrower gauge would suffice for such secondary railways in areas of light potential traffic.

As it was, the Culm Valley became a classic case of an under capitalised, under costed but overspent project, such has abounded from the earliest days of civil engineering to the present day. If the only debt had been the debentures, the CVLR would have lasted longer as an independent company and, if dissatisfied with the GWR's running of the line, the directors could perhaps have raised funds for locomotives and carriage stock to operate it themselves in the manner they intended. To have achieved this, Pain's choice of contractor and his supervision should have been better to enable the line to have been completed within the estimated cost. However, one suspects that Pain's ideas of building a railway for little more than £3,000 a mile in the 1870s was a little optimistic and probably reflected his inexperience.

The Whitland & Taf Vale Railway had been built for a modest £3,000 per mile but that figure excluded land and rolling stock. Pain had claimed the Swindon & Highworth Light Railway could be built for £4,000 per mile including land but its 5½ miles had cost £45,800 when it was taken over, unfinished, by the GWR. When they had completed it the cost had risen to £78,872. The Sidmouth Railway, albeit more heavily engineered, had authorised capital and borrowing powers totalling £88,000

for its 8½ miles length. A figure of £53,000 sufficed for the slightly longer Southwold Railway but, whilst its engineering was light and it was of narrow gauge, it had to purchase its own locomotives and rolling stock. Comparisons with other railways are not easy but do indicate that the final cost of the CVLR at a little over £6,000 per mile was, in fact, relatively cheap.

In Pain's favour one has to say that, ultimately, after the halts had been opened at Coldharbour and Whitehall, when the line had stopping places at almost every public road and when sidings served those local industries that needed rail transport, the line did resemble his original concept.

As for the impact the CVLR had on the valley, the numbers of passengers and tons of goods speak volumes. Only four or five passenger trains a day were run and most of the time the goods traffic was sufficient to be tacked on to these. The valley was a reasonably prosperous agricultural district and remained so, little changed by the new transport. The reintroduction of the quarterly market at Uffculme was one direct result, as was the Culm Davy brickworks. The latter, however, was unsuccessful and made little contribution to either the valley economy or the railway. William Furze's Uffculme Brewery did not take advantage of the new communication to turn the town into a rival to Burton on Trent but the railway may well have had an impact in the growth of the agricultural industries at Tiverton Junction, either directly or through the one successful industry that it did inspire. That was the Culm Valley Dairy, whose founders were astute enough to realise the value of good transport facilities. The dairy, later known as the milk factory, was a direct result of the railway and the reason for its survival. When the milk factory closed, so did the railway.

As we have noted, as the CVLR was constructing Arthur Pain became involved in other projects involving light or secondary railways. The first was the standard gauge Swindon & Highworth Light Railway, first mooted in September 1873. Its Act was passed in 1875 and the GWR agreed to work the line but construction did not start until 1879. Colonel Yolland's inspection in 1881 revealed £9,000 of work needed doing and, unable to afford this, the company sold out to the GWR. The line opened in 1883. Some parallels with the CVLR are apparent, especially in Yolland's criticism of the ballasting, short platforms and signalling arrangements, as well as in the finances.

Pain's other project at this time was the Southwold Railway, in Suffolk, and this narrow gauge railway proceeded rather more smoothly. The first public meeting was held in October 1875, the Act obtained in 1876 and the line opened in September 1879 after eighteen months' construction work. One suspects the choice of gauge and the lack of arrangements with a main line company were a direct result of Pain's experiences with his two standard gauge lines.

After this busy but not too fortunate start to his career in railway promotion Pain seems to have concentrated on other fields. As well as involvement in water works in the Home Counties, he took a leading part in local government in Surrey, where he lived. For a few years at the end of the 1870s he had been involved with Ellis and Newton in the Torbay & Brixham Railway and the Seaton & Beer Railway. On his own he was engineer from 1877 to 1880 to the Ely & Bury St Edmunds Railway, a line that was never built. Involvement with Newton came again in the 1890s in the Tottenham & Forest Gate Railway, which opened in 1894 and connected with the London Tilbury & Southend Railway. Other light railway work returned during the 1890s when a standard gauge branch to the Southwold Railway was proposed and, successfully, with his sons as assistants, he was engineer to the Axminster & Lyme Regis Light Railway. This standard gauge line obtained its Light Railway Order in 1899 and was opened in 1903 with considerable support from the LSWR. It was worked by them from the outset and was taken over in 1907. He remained engineer of the Southwold Railway until 1912 when he resigned in favour of his son, Claude, but was chairman of the company from 1903 until it closed, afflicted by road competition, in 1929. Arthur Pain died in 1937, aged 93.

Cecil Newton also went on to have an interesting career in railways. As has been noted, he

Arthur Cadlick Pain, taken in his later years, when he was prominent in local government in Surrey.

SIMON PAIN

had involvements in several independent Devon branch lines but ceased all such activity in 1882 on becoming secretary of the London Tilbury & Southend Railway, a position he retained until that company was taken over by the Midland Railway in 1912. He was also an auditor of the Grand Trunk Railway of Canada.

The question remains of whether the Culm Valley Light Railway was a success. As a pioneer light railway, perhaps not, nor as a branch of the GWR empire, but as a 'character' on the British railway stage it was eminently successful. It did make its own contribution, in a minor way, to a pleasant Devon valley and, by being unorthodox and non-standard, contributed to what we now call 'the quality of life.' A part of the valley life, it was an endearing and delightful railway and is remembered with great affection by those who knew and used it. Nothing more need be said.

At the end of the line as it nears the end of its days. D2119 pauses at Hemyock alongside the still waters of the river Culm. 30 April 1967.

M. J. MESSENGER

APPENDIX ONE:

Chronology

1844 May 1	B&ER opened through Tiverton Junction to Exeter.
1848 June 12	Tiverton branch opened (broad guage).
1868	Regulation of Railways Act.
1872 May 15	First meeting to propose the CVLR.
1873 May 15	Culm Valley Light Railway Act.
1876 March	Third rail laid on main line through to Exeter.
1876 May 29	CVLR opened for all traffic.
1876 June 1	Formal opening.
1877 June	Coldharbour and Culm Davey sidings approved and opened.
1880 August 5	CVLR sold to GWR.
1886	Culm Valley Dairy Company founded.
1916	United Daries take over CVDC.
1919 October 9	Uffculme private siding agreement, with Mr W. J. Williams.
1920 July 17	Hemyock private siding agreement, with United Dairies Ltd.
1929 February 23	Coldharbour Halt opened.
1933 February 27	Whitehall Halt opened.
1963 September 7	All passenger services withdrawn. Coldharbour, Culmstock and Whitehall closed for all purposes.
1965 September 6	Hemyock closes for all purposes except private siding (milk factory) traffic.
1967 May 8	Uffculme closes for all purposes except private siding traffic.
1975 October 31	Milk factory closes. Last train from Hemyock.

APPENDIX TWO:

Locomotives working on the CVLR

GWR	Origin	Built	On branch	Wdn/Scr	Wheels	Driving Wheel Diameter	Weight
1376	B&ER 114	1874	1876-1881	1934	0-6-0T*	3'6"	20T 8C
1377	B&ER 115	1875	1876-1881	1927	0-6-0T*	3'6"	20T 8C
1298	SDR	1878	1881-1926	1926	2-4-0T	4'0"	22T 12C
1300	SDR	1878	1881-1934	1934	2-4-0T	4'0"	22T 12C
1385	W&TVR 1	1872	c1895	1912+	0-6-0ST*	3'6"	26T 1C
1384	W&PRR 2	1876	c1906/11	1911+	2-4-0T	4'2"	24T 7C
1192	CRs 57	1866	1928-1929	1929	2-4-0T	4'6"	33T 3C
1196	CRs 58	1866	1927-1928	1948	2-4-0T	4'6"	33T 3C
1308	LLR	1902	1929	1948	2-4-0T	4'0"	32T
48xx	GWR	1932	1932-1966		0-4-2T	5'2"	41T 6C
204hp	BR	1957	1963		0-6-0DM		

Notes:
* May have worked as 0-4-2
+ Sold out of service

APPENDIX THREE:

Timetable summary

Date:	From Tiverton Junction							From Hemyock					
1876	6.50	9.35		12.40	4.30	6.45		8.30	10.35		3.00	5.25	7.45
1877	7.15	9.35		1240	4.30	6.30	5.50	8.30	10.35		3.00	5.30	
2/1879		9.30		12.50	4.25	6.30	9.25	8.30	10.30		2.50	5.20	8.20
10/1879		9.25		12.50	4.25	6.25		8.30	10.30		2.35	5.20	
1886		9.25		12.30	4.25	7.35		8.30	10.30		2.35	5.20	
3/1891		9.30		12.45	4.18	7.50		8.30	10.28		2.35	5.05	
10/1920		9.00		12.10	4.00	6.35		7.45	11.00		2.50	5.25	
1923		9.00		12.00	4X25	7.05		7.45	10.45		3.05	5.45	
6/1926		8.50	U		4.30	6.55		7.50	C		2.45	5.40	
W/1926		8.50	11.40	12.50	4.30	7.00		7.50	10.25	12.00	2.45	5.40	
9/1928	6F20 8.45	11.40	12.50	4.30	7.00	5F30	7.44	10.25	12.10	2.45	5.40		
1929		8.45	11.40	12.50	4.40	7.00	9$00	7.42	10.25	12.10	2.45	5.40	8$10
S/1930		8.45	11.40	12.50	4.40	7.00	9$05	7.35	10.35	12.10	2.45	5.40	8.10
S/1936		8.45	11.40	12.50	4.35	7.00	9$10	7.30	10.30	12.10	2.35	5.50	8.05 10$00
1947		8.45	11.35	1.30	4.32	7.10		7.30	10.30	12.10	3.00	5.55	8.08
1948	5F50 8.45	11.35	1.35	4.33	7.10		7.30	10.30	12.10	3.00	5.55	8.08	
1963		8*45	11.25	1.42	5.10			7.10	10.30	12.20	2.45	6.00	

Notes: $ – Saturday only. * – except Saturday, 9$20. X – except Saturday, 4$40. U to Uffculme.
C – from Culmstock. W – Winter timetable. S – Summer timetable. F – Freight working

APPENDIX FOUR:

List of Shareholders (as at the cessation of the CVLR Company)

SURNAME	FIRST NAMES	OCCUPATION	ADDRESS	COUNTY	SHARES
Ashford	Charles	Accountant	Exeter	Devon	10
Babb	George	Innkeeper	Hemyock	Devon	1
Barnes	Samuel	Solicitor	Bellair, Exeter	Devon	10
Barnes	William		Great Duryard, Exeter	Devon	10
Barnes	William, Jnr		The Grove, Mt Radford, Exeter	Devon	25
Barrow	John James		35 Westbourne Terrace, W.	London	10
Barter	Edwin James		26 Quadrant Grove, London N.W.	London	10
Barton	George	Yeoman	Hemyock	Devon	5
Battishall	William John	Solicitor	Exeter	Devon	10
Bevan	Richard D.		Uffculme	Devon	2
Beverley	Richard		8 Brownswood Pk. South, Hornsey	London	10
Blackmore	William	Yeoman	The Palmers, Clayhidon	Devon	2
Bowerman	Richard John	Solicitor	3 Grays Inn Square	London	68
Brent	Sarah & Julia	Spinsters	Topsham	Devon	10
Brimblecombe	Henry	Accountant	Exeter	Devon	10
Broom	J.	Farmer	Culmstock	Devon	1
Burrow	Frederick	deceased	Cullompton	Devon	2
Clist	George	Farmer	Hemyock	Devon	1
Collins	Charles R.	Manufacture	Strathculm, Cullompton	Devon	25
Corner	Richard	Printer	The Bower, Wellington	Somerset	1
Cotton	William	Banker	The Close, Exeter	Devon	10
Cridland	George	Yeoman	The Greys, Clayhidon	Devon	2
Cridland	Robert	Yeoman	The Greys, Clayhidon	Devon	1
Dansic	Thomas French		26 Throgmorton St, London E.C.	London	10
Driver	Charles H.		5 Victoria Street S.W.	London	2
Dunsford	Francis	Banker	Tiverton	Devon	5
Durrant	Richard	deceased			50
Edwards, Rev	Henry		Chuchstaunton	Devon	5
Ellis	Mary Ann, Mrs	Widow	67 Ladbrooke Grove Road, W.	London	100
Ellis	Henry	Farmer	Hemyock	Devon	1
Ensor, Rev	Frederick		Lustleigh, Newton Abbot	Devon	10
Farmer	Joseph	Farmer	Newest, Clayhidon	Devon	1
Farrant	Edward	Yeoman	New House, Hemyock	Devon	10
Farrant	Elizabeth	Widow	Holcombe, Hemyock	Devon	1
Farrant	Henry	Yeoman	Culmstock	Devon	1
Farrant	Samuel	Yeoman	Dunkeswell, Honiton	Devon	5
Farrant	John	Yeoman	Hemyock	Devon	10
Fisher	William	Innkeeper	Tiverton	Devon	2

SURNAME	FIRST NAMES	OCCUPATION	ADDRESS	COUNTY	SHARES
Follett	Charles John	Solicitor	78 Queens Gate, S.W.	London	30
Follett, Lt. Col.	Robert Wm. Webb	Coldstream Guards	Windsor	Berkshire	31
Follett & Furze			78 Queens Gate, S.W.	London	43
Ford	Charles T.	Farmer	Stoke Cannon, Exeter	Devon	10
Forrester	Henry		23 Throgmorton Street E.C	London	10
Frecker	Frederick Farrow		Ridgway, Wimbledon	Surrey	10
Furze	William	Brewer	Uffculme	Devon	510
Gear	Charles	Accountant	Addiscombe, Croydon	Surrey	10
Gill	Henry S.		Tiverton	Devon	10
Graham	Edward	Storekeeper	Culmstock	Devon	1
Graham	John Laurence		Pinner, Middlesex	Middx	10
Great Western	Rly Co.		Paddington, W.	London	400
Green	Ernest Richard		23 Throgmorton Street, E.C.	London	10
Houlditch	Edward Holroyd	Solicitor	Exeter	Devon	10
Johnson	Robert Channon		Belmont Place, Exeter	Devon	10
Karslake, Rev.	John W.		Culmstock	Devon	8
Keen	Arthur	Managing Director	London Works, Birmingham	Warwick	10
Knollys	Henry Francis		Exeter	Devon	10
Knowlman	J. C. Jnr	Yeoman	Culmstock	Devon	1
Lane	John		Tiverton	Devon	10
Langdon	James H	Contractor	Williton	Somerset	8
Lutley	Edward	Merchant	Hemyock	Devon	33
Lutley	Edward Jnr	Miller	Hemyock	Devon	1
Outred	Thomas		14 Austin Friars, E.C.	London	10
Pain	Arthur C.	(Engineer)	5 Victoria Street, S.W.	London	103
Pain	Robert T		Snowdenham, Bromley	Kent	8
Pain	Coard S.		4 Cook Street, Liverpool		6
Pain	Wm. H. B.		171 Marylebone Road, N.W.	London	5
Pollard	William	Printer	North Street, Exeter	Devon	15
Porter	Henry Aylmer		Holcombe, Dawlish	Devon	10
Porter	Charlotte M.		Holcombe, Dawlish	Devon	10
Porter	George Adrian		The Buffs, Shorncliffe	Sussex	9
Ransome & Rapier			Ipswich	Suffolk	7
Rew	Charles Henry		5 Victoria Street, S.W.	London	1
Richards	William Joseph	Wine Merchant	Queen Street, Exeter	Devon	5
Row	William North		Tiverton	Devon	10
Rowcliffe	Charles		Stogumber	Somerset	10
Sampson	William		26 Throgmorton Street, E.C.	London	10
Seymour	George		Exeter	Devon	10
Snow	Thomas M.		Cleeves, Exeter	Devon	15
Southey	George	Maltster	Uffculme	Devon	5
Still	Charles George		10 St. Oswalds Rd, W. Brompton	London	10
Stokes	Thomas	Gardener	Franklyn, Exeter	Devon	2
Sully	George B.		Bridgewater (sic)	Somerset	25

SURNAME	FIRST NAMES	OCCUPATION	ADDRESS	COUNTY	SHARES
Tapscott	Henry	Merchant	Fore Street, Exeter	Devon	11
Taylor	Robert H.	Banker	Tiverton	Devon	5
Temple	The Rt. Rev. Frederic	Lord Bishop of Exeter	The Palace, Exeter	Devon	30
Thomas	Henry Drew		Exeter	Devon	35
Thomas	J. Langdon		Exeter	Devon	5
Trobridge	Jas. Townsend		Exeter	Devon	10
Tucker	John	Yeoman	Hemyock	Devon	5
Varley	O. & F. H.	Telegraph Contractors	Mildmay Avenue, Highbury	London	2
Wakeford	William		11 Great George Street	London	10
Walrond	Sir John W.	Bart	Bradfield House, Cullompton	Devon	25
Walton	James		6 Great College Street	London	4
Ware	James	Coliery Owner	Cardiff	Glamorgan	60
West	Sarah, Mrs		Streatham Hall, Exeter	Devon	120
Wide	James	Storekeeper	Hemyock	Devon	1
Wide	John	Storekeeper	Hemyock	Devon	1
Wilcocks	Henry	Merchant	Spurlburne, Exeter	Devon	10
Wildman	Thomas		Custom House	London	10

Distribution of the 103 Shareholders of the CVLR, at the company's cessation.

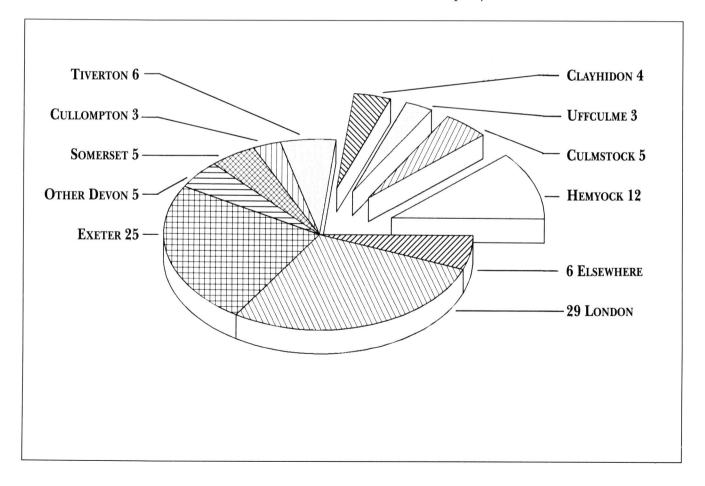

ACKNOWLEDGEMENTS AND SOURCES

Writing history can be a solitary occupation – whether poring over archive material in library or record office – or hunched over the keyboard drawing the strands together to make a logical and convincing story. Nevertheless, many other people must contribute in a number of ways to a narrative such as this, for only the most insufferable person could claim sufficient knowledge of all the facets that come to light in even a relatively simple branch line history.

Firstly, one's friends ply one with useful snippets and helpful suggestions. Secondly there are the friends and contacts with specialised knowledge that one makes use of. Thirdly, there are the professional archivists, curators and librarians who cheerfully embrace the stranger's request for obscure information.

In the last category the staff of all the establishments listed below have without exception been most helpful and accommodating, and one's letters or visits to their premises have inevitably been met in a most rewarding way: British Library, Brunel University Library, Cardiff City Library, Devon Record Office (Exeter), House of Lords Record Office, Institute of Agricultural History (University of Reading), The Institution of Civil Engineers, Leicester University Library, Public Record Office (Kew), Railway Correspondence & Travel Society Library, Royal Institution of Cornwall, Tiverton Museum, University of Wales College of Cardiff (Aberconway Library), West Country Studies Library (Exeter).

Particular thanks must go to my friends in the Railway & Canal Historical Society; Grahame Boyes, Harry Paar, Don Steggles and Alan Voce. How fortunate, and useful, it has been that Alan Voce should have become deeply involved in Tiverton Museum Society, with as a consequence an intimate knowledge of their archive, and that Don Steggles should have become responsible for Devon Library's Railway Studies Library at Newton Abbot.

Many other people have helped in a variety of ways and I formally record my appreciation here, in alphabetical order to save any invidious favouritism, to R. H. Alford, Simon Bowditch, Amyas Crump, Alan Dixon, Gordon Green (Industrial Railway Society), Alan A. Jackson, R. W. Kidner, David M. Lee, Simon and Jane Pain, Frank D. Smith, Anthony Taylor, Chris Tilley, Russell Wear.

Photographers are acknowledged under each photograph but especial thanks must be given to Richard Casserley and R. C. Riley. Help with the illustrations has also come from David Assar, John Stengelhofen and Alan Kittridge, the last named also designing this book. Grahame Boyes read the manuscript and I am most grateful, as the reader should be, for his close attention to detail.

Sources

Fortunately the official records of most railway companies survive and it is the Culm Valley Light Railway Directors' minutes that have provided the bare bones of this story. It is fleshed out from the Board of Trade files and from the records of the other companies that were involved, the Bristol & Exeter Railway and the Great Western Railway. Clothes and life came from contemporary accounts in local newspapers and other journals, whether relating the current scene or reminiscing past events
Main archival and other sources are listed below:

Public Record Office, Kew:
RAIL 147/1 CVLR Directors' Minute Book
RAIL 147/3 CVLR Shareholders List
RAIL 147/8-9 CVLR Correspondence files
RAIL 147/10 CVLR Traffic Returns
RAIL 147/11 CVLR Ball Ticket
RAIL 1075/89 CVLR Prospectus
RAIL 1110/93 CVLR Reports and accounts
RAIL 75/46, 48 B&ER Directors' Minute Books
RAIL 250/30, 55 GWR Directors' Minute Books
RAIL 250/169, 180-181 GWR Engineering
Committee Minutes

RAIL 250/354-357 GWR Traffic Committee Minutes
RAIL 250/715 GWR Traffic Research Committee, Exeter District 1936-37
RAIL 250/736 GWR Report on Branch Lines 1926
RAIL 266/45 GWR Station statistics
RAIL 274/116 GWR Survey
MT6 157/18 Board of Trade papers CVLR 1875-76
MT6 181/5 Board of Trade papers CVLR 1877
MT6 1079/1 Board of Trade papers GWR 1902
BT31 2657/14147 Company records, Culm Davy Brick & Tile Co. Ltd.
BT31 31127/27759 Company records, Culm Valley Dairy Co. Ltd.
BT31 4131/2627 Upper Culm Valley Dairy Company, and Farmers' Association, Ltd.
BT31 13638/116386 Hemyock Sone & Coal Co. Ltd.

Devon Record Office:
113A/205/6 Quarter Sessions 1877
74B/MB14 Highways Board 1872-5
1926 B/FO/B 1/1-2 Culm Davy Brickworks

Acts:
36Vic.c.xxv The Culm Valley Light Railway Act 1873
37-8Vic.c.xxiii The Bristol & Exeter Railway Act 1874
38-9Vic.c.cxxvii The Bristol & Exeter Railway Act 1875

Newspapers & Magazines:
Devon & Somerset News
Exeter Flying Post
Great Western Railway Magazine
Railway Observer
Tiverton Gazette & East Devon Herald
Tiverton Times

Articles:
Anon. 'Hemyock Branch'. *Railway Observer*, 1963, 343–44.

Cooper, B. K. 'The Culm Valley Branch of the GWR'. *Railway Magazine*, 1936, 116–20, 423–26.

Cooper, B. K. 'Culm Valley–a memoir'. *Railway World*, Vol. 37, 1976, 106–8.

Gentry, P. W. 'The Culm Valley Light Railway'. *Railway World*, Vol. 14, 1953, 38–40, 119.

Karau, P. 'Common Light Railway Architecture'. *British Railway Journal*, No 1 October 1983.

Lutley, D. 'Culm Valley Memories'. *Railway Magazine*, 1987, 176–78.

Riley, R. C. 'The Culm Valley Branch'. *Railway World*, Vol. 23, 1962, 369–72.

Whetham, E. H. 'The London milk trade, 1860–1900'. *Economic History Review*, 2nd series. Vol. XVII, 1964, 369–80.

Bibliography:
Bradshaw's Railway Shareholders Manual, various dates

Clinker, C.R. *Clinker's Register of Closed Stations.*

Dracott, Chris & Clist, Brian. *Hemyock, A village history*, Hemyock [1986]

Forrester, R. B. *The Fluid Milk Market in England & Wales*, Ministry of Agriculture Fisheries & Food, Economic Series 16 1927

Holden, J. S. *The Manchester & Milford Railway*, Tarrant Hinton 1979

Karau, Paul. *Great Western Branch Line Termini, Volume 2*, Oxford 1978

Kelly's Directory of Devon, various dates

McDermot, E. T. *History of the Great Western Railway, Volume 2 1863-1921*, Revised edition 1964

Pain, Arthur C. *Light Railways and Tramroads*, 1873

Price, M. R. C. *The Whitland & Cardigan Railway*, Tarrant Hinton 1976

Railways Clearing House, *Handbook of Stations*, various dates

The Locomotives of the Great Western Railway, Part 3, Absorbed Engines 1854-1921, Railway Correspondence & Travel Society 1956

The Locomotives of the Great Western Railway, Part 10, Absorbed Engines 1922-1947, Railway Correspondence & Travel Society 1966

Sainsbury, Peter. *The Transition from Tradition to Technology, a history of the dairy industry in Devon*, Tiverton 1991

Smith, T. M. & Heathcliffe, G. S. *The Highworth Branch*, Didcot 1979

Taylor, Alan R. & Tonks, Eric S. *The Southwold Railway*, Shepperton n.d.

Taylor, Anthony. *Culm Valley Album*, Author 1987

Thomas, David St.J. *A Regional History of the Railways of Great Britain, Volume 1 - The West Country*, 1960

Uffculme, a Culm Valley Parish, Uffculme Local History Group 1988

Whetham, E. M. *The London Milk Trade 1900–1930*, Research Papers No. 2, Institute of Agricultural History, University of Reading 1970.

INDEX

A selection of tickets from the Hemyock branch. Clockwise from the top left they are dated 12 June 1959, 5 January 1963, 7 September 1963, 1 November 1975, 7 September 1963 and 24 August 1963. Two were issued on the last day of passenger service but that at bottom right is of particular interest as it was prepared for a planned special last train that did not run, due to the progress of the motorway works that would cut off the line.

COLLECTION AMYAS CRUMP

West of Hemyock, the track lifting gang have passed by, removing the rails to one side and leaving the sleepers turned over, all to be picked up on the next visit. After more than one hundred years the Culm Valley Light Railway had, to paraphrase Charles Follett's remarks of 1881, finally ceased to exist.

CHRIS TILLEY